Emma Eames as Amelia at the Met., 1905 (private collection)

Preface

This series, launched in 1980 by English National Opera, is made possible by generous sponsorship. We are most grateful for the continuing support of Martini and Rossi Ltd, who have also sponsored the Opera Guides to *Madam Butterfly* and *Macbeth*. Their interest enables us to commission and publish new research and up-to-date English performing translations in volumes with a wide circulation which reach opera-lovers all over the world. We hope that, as companions to the opera should be, they are well-informed, witty and attractive.

Nicholas John
Series Editor

40

A Masked Ball
Un ballo in maschera

Giuseppe Verdi

Opera Guide Series Editor: Nicholas John

This guide is sponsored by Martini and Rossi Ltd

Published in association with
English National Opera

 John Calder · London
Riverrun Press · New York

First published Great Britain, 1989 by
John Calder (Publishers) Ltd,
18 Brewer Street,
London W1R 4AS

First published in the USA, 1989, by
Riverrun Press Inc.,
1170 Broadway,
New York, NY 10001.

Copyright © English National Opera 1989
'The Fusion of Styles' © Pierluigi Petrobelli 1989
'A King Restored: Structure and Music in "A Masked Ball"' © Benedict Sarnaker 1989
'The "Laughing Chorus" in Contexts' © Harold Powers 1989
'A Masked Ball' English translation © Edmund Tracey 1989

BRITISH LIBRARY CATALOGUING IN PUBLICATION DATA
Verdi, Giuseppe, *1813-1901*
    A masked ball.—(Opera Guide series; 40).
    1. Opera in Italian—Librettos—Italian-English parallel texts
    I. Title   II. Series
782.1'2

ISBN 0 7145 4167 2

LIBRARY OF CONGRESS CATALOGING IN PUBLICATION DATA
Verdi, Giuseppe, 1813-1901.
    [Ballo in maschera. Libretto. English & Italian]
    Un ballo in maschera / Giuseppe Verdi.
        p.   cm.—(Opera guide: 40)
    Includes libretto in Italian by Antonio Somma based on Scribe's
libretto for Auber's Gustave III, with English translation.
    "Published in association with English National Opera."
    Includes bibliographical references.
    Discography: p. 93
    ISBN 0-7145-4167-2 (pbk.) : $7.95
    1. Operas—Librettos. 2. Verdi, Giuseppe, 1813-1901. Ballo in
maschera. I. Somma, Antonio, 1809-1864. II. Scribe, Eugène, 1791-1861. Gustave III.
III. English National Opera House (London, England) IV. Title.
ML50.V484B22 1989 <Case>
781.1—dc20   89-10650
                                                                  CIP
                                                                   MN

Typeset in Plantin by Maggie Spooner Typesetting, London
Printed in Great Britain by The Camelot Press, Southampton

Contents

List of Illustrations

Cover design: Anita Boyd

Frontispiece: Emma Eames as Amelia at the Met., 1905 (private collection)

Picture research by Ian Stones

Introduction

Nicholas John

When writing for the Teatro San Carlo in Naples under the Bourbon régime, any composer would have expected problems with the authorities. Verdi's choice in 1857 of a libretto dealing with political assassination was obviously provocative. It hardly mattered that the basis for the new Italian libretto was a twenty-five-year-old French text, which had already been played over 150 times at the Paris opera with Auber's music. Nor that the appeal of this subject — the murder of Gustavus III of Sweden — was infinitely more profound for a composer and a librettist who had just been collaborating on a draft of *King Lear* (never composed) than its political context.

Gustavus was shot by a nobleman, one Anckarstroem, at a masked ball in the Stockholm opera house in 1792. Antonio Somma, Verdi's librettist, based his version on that of Eugène Scribe's *Gustave III ou Le bal masqué*, set to music by Auber in 1833. Scribe had drawn much of his information from the French translation of John Brown's very colourful survey of *The Northern Courts; Original Memoirs of the Sovereigns of Sweden and Denmark* (London, 1818), written when it was, after all, quite recent history. Here he found an acid description of the charismatic Gustavus, famous for his delight in theatricals, for his visits to Mademoiselle Arvidson the fortune-teller, and for his popularity with the people. Among many telling anecdotes, Brown observes how the arrival of a royal page with invitations to a court ball would successfully divert the complaints of the ladies of Stockholm from grumbling at breakfast about the taxes. He also vividly describes the place of public execution when he tells of the terrible punishments inflicted on Anckarstroem.

Scribe adopted the Swedish location, with some of the deputies in the authentic National dress which Gustavus himself designed, and French revolutionary sentiments among the plotters. But he pointedly ignored the main theme of Brown's vitriolic characterisation of Gustavus III. Far from being a ladies' man, the historical figure was a homosexual; as Brown puts it, 'he did not pay homage at the shrine of Venus' but surrounded himself with 'voluptuous and depraved parasites, such as might be expected to abound in an Asiatic court.' Scribe invented a romantic entanglement more appropriate for the Parisian operatic stage.

Verdi and Somma had to deal with the Bourbon censors before their opera could be performed in Naples. Seven initial stipulations were made: 1, the King must become a duke; 2, the action must be transferred to a pre-Christian age when witchcraft and the summoning-up of spirits were believed in; 3, anywhere in the North would do except for Norway and Sweden; 4, the hero's love must be noble and tinged with remorse; 5, the conspirators must hate the duke for hereditary reasons such as usurpation of property; 6, the feast should conform to the customs of the epoch chosen; 7, no firearms. After considerable argument they agreed on seventeenth-century Pomerania, and to call it *Una vendetta in domino* (*A Masked Revenge*).

When Verdi submitted his finished libretto in January 1858, however, there had just been an assassination attempt in Paris on Napoleon III (January 13), and the censors referred the matter to the Chief of Police, who decreed that the whole text would have to be rewritten. The management produced *Adeglia*

7

degli Adimari, set in fourteenth-century Florence; Verdi refused to have anything to do with it, and withdrew in a flurry of lawsuits.

Already in February 1858 Verdi was fishing for a production in Rome. The Roman censor demanded different alterations, making Riccardo the Count of Gothenburg. Now Somma objected, arguing that this was 'merely caprice'. In the end the censor made less alterations than foreseen, although he demanded that the location should be moved away from Europe and that Riccardo should not be a Duke. Verdi suggested 'North America at the time of the English domination' and that Riccardo should become 'Conte di Warwich', and this was the final solution. The character list also mentions that Renato is a 'creole' but it is unclear what this means. By September 1858 Verdi had decided that the libretto even gained by the changes but Somma refused to put his name to it. It was performed in its Boston setting all over Europe, except at the Théâtre-Lyrique in Paris in 1861, where the action was moved to Italy. Because designers had no reference source for seventeenth-century Boston, this usually meant costumes which owed their inspiration to Mercadante's *The Regent*, a previous Italian version of the Scribe libretto, which had been relocated to sixteenth-century Scotland. The scene of the masked ball, however, was usually more akin to contemporary opera balls.

Because Verdi never rejected the North American setting, productions have reflected designers' attempts to come to grips with the underlying tension between the action and this location. There is much to be said in favour of reverting to Somma's original text, and this was first done for a Danish translation in Copenhagen in 1935. In 1952 E.J. Dent prepared an English version for Covent Garden, restoring Scribe's names. In 1959 Erik Lindegren's Swedish version for the Royal Swedish Opera went even further by attempting to impose historical accuracy upon the libretto. Here the King's affair with Amelia is merely a front for his real interest in his page, renamed Otto. Anckarstroem is not the King's friend, Renato, but Ribbing; Renato is renamed Holberg, the historical minister. This involves a complicated manoeuvre at the end when Anckarstroem is arrested for a murder which Holberg has actually committed.

When the opera was first given in 1965 by Sadler's Wells, in a production by Glen Byam Shaw, and translation by Leonard Hancock, the Swedish setting was adopted, as it has been in this new English translation for English National Opera. The Opera Guide articles, however, use the more generally familiar Italian names to refer to the characters, as in the score. Confusing as it may seem, there is, we hope, some sense in this arrangement.

The Fusion of Styles

Pierluigi Petrobelli

I bought Verdi's *A Masked Ball* to have a few hours of company. It's a strong, brutal work of great force and plasticity. It seems to me that some passages in this opera can be counted among the best in Verdi. I did not know it before but have discovered many things in it which are familiar to me from childhood. But what a libretto! And the verses! It is the story of Gustavus III transferred to Boston, for political reasons. 'Odo l'orma dei passi spietati' [*lit.* I hear the fall of merciless footsteps] — Has one ever heard the like?

Thus wrote Ferruccio Busoni, pausing on one of his endless concert-tours, to his wife from Trento in July, 1906. It is a telling reaction since it expresses the ambivalent mood of a generation utterly divorced from the intellectual and artistic climate in which Verdi's opera was written, while at the same time it registers the response of a brilliant musician who instinctively grasped its essence, however far removed from his own attitude and sensitivity.

Busoni's attitude is neither isolated nor uncommon. On the contrary, I would say that it is a constant factor in the fortunes of the opera, almost up to the present. The fact is that *A Masked Ball* represents a unique and unrepeatable moment in Verdi's art. Simplistic definitions cannot comfortably pin it down. Far from corresponding to the expectations which it might seem to invite, this opera undermines them. Whoever wants an unfolding of broad, simple melody in the so-called Italian tradition may be satisfied by 'O qual soave brivido' but will find it hard to accept pieces like 'È scherzo od è follia' or 'Saper vorreste' — built on short, self-contained melodic cells which are developed in a way absolutely foreign to that tradition. On the other hand, a listener who is trained to respond to and enjoy subtleties of harmony and timbre will, with good reason, find whole sections hard to take, such as the finales of the first Act and the band music in the last.

The differences — some would say the contradictions — styles in this opera can be best appreciated if we consider the creative period in Verdi's career to which it belongs.

With *The Sicilian Vespers* (1855), Verdi for the first time confronted the complex experience of *grand opéra* independently, that is to say without having to adapt an existing score to the genre. He had to respect the inflexible conditions which had rapidly become customary for this genre of theatre — five Acts, a massive use of chorus, an obligatory ballet in the third Act, and in particular a vocal style devoted more to chiselled detail than to melodic expansion. *Grand opéra* offered opportunities to play with the subtleties of orchestration, both for solo instruments and for orchestral colour. It was a tempting challenge for Verdi: the rules of this style invited experimentation along avenues almost unexplored in the Italian tradition. The real problem, however, lay in the fact that the dramatic and musical conception that these experiments had to serve obeyed principles diametrically opposed to those which Verdi — stubbornly and in various forms — had developed over the years between *Macbeth* (1846-47) and *Il trovatore* (1853). The French tradition concentrated meticulous attention upon detail, polished 'avec bon goût' and presented 'comme il faut', to the detriment of a vision of the whole, or of an overall concept of musical drama. On the contrary, Verdi's scores reveal his constant and systematic striving for dramatic unity, achieved exclusively with musical means — notwithstanding the fact that he adopted different solutions for each opera, or that he almost always used conventional principles of musical organisation.

Pursuing his quest for a personal language, Verdi pushed the whole love story of *Simon Boccanegra* (1857) into the background, and in the foreground he placed opposing political concepts and individuals driven by complex and varied motivations. In *Boccanegra* the experience of *grand opéra* is not forgotten: significantly, when Verdi made his radical revision of the score in 1881, he rejected precisely those sections which most directly adhered to that genre. In the revision the drama is further enriched by conflicts, and consequently by musico-dramatic solutions, which have nothing to do with the French tradition.

In *A Masked Ball*, Verdi posed himself another problem. Here it is not so much the matter of conflicts which are unusual to the Italian tradition but rather the allotment of different styles to define different dramatic levels, all within the development of a single plot. In the story of Gustavus III of Sweden, as treated by Scribe in a *drame lyrique* for Auber which had its first stage performance at the Académie Royale de la Musique on February 27, 1833, the protagonist's character could not be depicted with the usual attributes of the young lover (i.e. the tenor) of Italian opera. Not only does the young sovereign love the wife of his most faithful subject — which in itself generates an internal conflict and thus a continual fluctuation of 'affects' —but, most importantly, there is a 'light' side to him, a continual desire to play and to joke, which adds yet another dimension to his character. This 'light' side of Gustavus-Riccardo is best reflected in the character of Oscar. In a sense, Oscar is nothing more than the external projection of this aspect of his master's personality.

The other two main characters are no less complex. Amelia is constantly torn between an ever stronger feeling of love for Riccardo and at the same time remorse at her betrayal of her husband. Renato is at first utterly intent upon defending his master against the conspirators and then, once betrayal is revealed, equally intent upon revenge for the outrage he has suffered.

The social and political pressures which are added to the internal conflicts of these multifaceted characters also play a significant part in the overall shape of the drama. On the one hand, there is the generous magnanimity of Riccardo, the embodiment of an Enlightened eighteenth-century prince; on the other, the darkly calculating plotting of the conspirators, among whom Sam and Tom are merely the chorus leaders, restless subjects who cannot bear Riccardo's rule.

It is very difficult to discern in Auber's score, which is built on 'numbers' with stophic songs, any attempt to give dramatic individuality to the various situations in which the characters find themselves. As such, it is perfectly consistent with the French operatic tradition, with its usual attention to detail and its marked indifference to the construction of a whole musico-dramatic discourse. Only a few years later, in 1843, Saverio Mercadante set *Il reggente* (*The Regent*) to music. Modelled on the same text by Scribe, the action was transferred, because of the censor, to Scotland and the protagonist was no longer a prince. The musical language is rooted, however, in the Italian tradition, both as to the vocal style and to the whole articulation of the dramatic development. The central situations of the action are constantly highlighted and moments of great dramatic intensity are thereby created —

10

Enrico Caruso as Riccardo at the Met., 1905 (private collection)

particularly the 'invocation' of the fortune-teller Meg (who was to become Verdi's Ulrica). In spite of such moments, it seems to me that the composer was unable to find a musical equivalent to express the development of the drama. Although Mercadante's score is interesting in many ways and obviously created by a strong musical imagination, it lacks the definition yielded by incisive contrast; there is no tension in the musical rendering of the conflicts in the plot.

This is precisely what Verdi manages to do, from the very first bars of the score. In the orchestral Prelude the motif [1] characterising the love of Riccardo's subjects alternates with that of the conspirators' plotting [2], and both revolve around the theme of Riccardo's love for Amelia [3], the musical idea which truly does run through the opera — its 'recurrent theme'*. It is present in Riccardo's *aria di sortita* in the Introduction ('La rivedrò nell'estasi), and, significantly, in the orchestral opening to his last *romanza* ('Ma se m'è forza perderti') in the complex Finale of the third Act. The greatest contrast in the levels of musical language, however, is used to characterise the 'light' and 'dark' areas of the plot. On the 'light' side, there is the carefree young sovereign, his love of disguises, jokes and pranks — that part of his personality which finds its perfect incarnation in the character of Oscar. For this element in the score Verdi draws unhesitatingly on the French tradition, as much for the musical forms as for the musical language. Oscar has only two numbers entirely his own and both of them set music to a text of two stanzas: the first is the *ballata* 'Volta la terrea' [5] which, in the tradition of Hérold, Halévy, Auber and every other French composer, serves the purpose of telling the audience the antecedents of the plot. This occurs at the beginning of the opera, in the Introduction of the first Act. The second is at the end of the opera, in the *Finale terzo*: the *canzone* 'Saper vorreste' [32]. Both pieces play on melodic phrases that are short and complete in themselves, on a rapid succession of long intervals in the vocal line, with staccato notes and brilliant flourishes. It is the same musical style that characterises Riccardo's part in the Quintet at the end of Act One, 'È scherzo od è follia' [14], the climax of his high-spirited masquerade at Ulrica's dwelling.

On the 'dark' side, the relationships of love and jealousy in the eternal triangle are expressed according to the traditional rules of Italian opera. It is no mere chance that this situation is most completely realised in the central part of the drama: the brief, intense second Act, which contains a deliberately compressed series of 'situations' connected by the deepest dramatic tension. As opposed to the complex structure of the first and third Acts, the linear simplicity of this pivotal part of the action is very striking: Amelia's aria, the Amelia-Riccardo duet, the Amelia-Riccardo-Renato trio and finally, after the identification, the quartet (Amelia, Renato, Sam and Tom) with the chorus. It opens on an empty stage with only the spectral presence of the gallows, and closes as the mocking laughter of the conspirators fades away into the emptiness of the night. In this bitterly ironic comment on the twist of the plot, the musical echo of the French tradition can be clearly heard.

Both of the outer Acts are subdivided into two parts (with consequent scene-changes): the first opens with a long Introduction of many sections, corresponding to Scribe's entire Act One, which brings out some of the basic

---

* In the sense of Joseph Kerman's essay 'Verdi's use of recurring themes' in *Studies in Music History: Essays for Oliver Strunk*, ed. Harold Powers, Princeton, 1968; pp 495-510.

Thérèse Tietjens, the first Amelia in Britain at the Lyceum in 1861. Rosina Penco sang the role twelve days later at Covent Garden. (Royal College of Music)

elements in the plot: the figure of Riccardo and the dual reaction (of love and hatred) of his subjects towards him; the faithfulness of Renato, and the light-hearted nonchalance of Oscar. The much longer and more complex second part introduces the tormented anxiety of Amelia but above all develops the 'light' aspect of Riccardo's character. Likewise, the third Act has a long first part which takes place in Renato's house and which hinges upon the plot to kill Riccardo, with the scene when the names are extracted from the urn as the focal point of the action. It ends, however, with an identical structure to the opening: a long *Finale terzo* in many sections, which corresponds exactly to Scribe's Act Five. I would like to conclude by calling attention to the perfect balance of symmetries, correspondences and parallels on which this opera is built.

In *A Masked Ball*, Verdi aims at underlining the complexity of the theatrical message, and even the ambiguities it involves. For this reason, his return to Scribe's original subtitle should not be dismissed as coincidental. He chose it (rejecting a title like *Una vendetta in domino* — *A Masked Revenge* — which would have been too simplistic) so as not to emphasise this or that aspect of the

13

Tom Swift as Gustavus and Rita Hunter as Amelia in the production at the London Coliseum in 1974 (photo: John Garner)

plot but only its tragic, ambivalent conclusion. In that conclusion, the play of contrasts, of the 'light' against the 'serious', of day and night, of friendship that turns to jealousy, of conjugal fidelity which struggles with love, of a loyalty towards the most faithful subject which must struggle with the more imperious emotion of love — all this finds its vivid and supreme manifestation in the contrast between the 'indifferent' sound of the three stage bands (the most refined and complex allusion, among the many in Verdi's operas, to the first Act finale of *Don Giovanni*) and the last desperate dialogue of the two lovers. Once more, this is a play within a play, but not as a pleasing and escapist intellectual *divertissement*, or as a pure release of fantasy, but rather as an implacable reading of the game of life, of the continuous coexistence in it of the serious and frivolous, the tragic and the light, the sublime and the vulgar. From this perspective we may finally succeed in understanding what Verdi really meant when he wrote to De Sanctis, speaking of 'subjects that are new, great, beautiful, passionate — passionate in the extreme . . .', adding that he would now refuse, if they were again proposed to him, subjects like those of *Nabucco* and *The Two Foscari*, since they were 'without variety', lacking, that is, internal conflicts. Never again would Verdi find the courage, which he had when he wrote *A Masked Ball*, to create tension between two poles so far apart. It is perhaps this which makes the opera so unique, and explains why we perceive this kind of musical theatre as so close to our sensibility.

A King Restored: Structure and music in 'A Masked Ball'

Benedict Sarnaker

Verdi had completed the radically inventive *Simon Boccanegra* and was exploring the project of *King Lear* in detail when, during the spring of 1856, he was approached by Vincenzo Torelli (the secretary to the management of the San Carlo theatre in Naples) with the offer of a contract. Despite Verdi's search for something new, time and other circumstances resulted in a superficially conventional and even hackneyed solution to this commission — a twenty-five-year-old French libretto which had already been set by three composers.

Eugène Scribe's libretto took the real, but obscurely motivated, assassination of Gustave III and arbitrarily added 'cherchez la femme' as a motive. With exuberant craftsmanship (and a sharp eye for the Parisian public which valued spectacle and sensation far more highly than the truthful portrayal of historical character) Scribe piled *coups de théâtre* on top of multiple ironies into the five highly-charged acts of *Gustave III, ou Le bal masqué*. This text was set by Daniel Auber and first performed in Paris in 1833.

Despite the presence of such great singers as Adolphe Nourrit in the role of Gustave, Cornélie Falcon as Amélie and Nicholas Levasseur as Ankastrom (sic), Auber's setting enjoyed only a modest success in France and abroad. Its music is too even-paced and soft-grained. The tender moments between Amélie (Verdi's Amelia) and Gustave (Riccardo) are effective, but tragedy is beyond his grasp. A year later Vincenzo Bellini was considering the subject, until his death snuffed out this fascinating project. Yet it continued to excite Italian operatic composers and in 1841 Vincenzo Gabussi produced his treatment (with an Italian libretto by Gaetano Rossi) at the Teatro la Fenice, Venice, under the title of *La Clemenza di Valois*. This work has little merit and has not held its place on stage. On the other hand, *Il reggente* (Teatro Reggio, Turin, 1843) the other pre-Verdian setting (on a text by Salvadore Cammarano, the librettist of Verdi's *Luisa Miller* and *Il trovatore* as well as Donizetti's *Lucia di Lammermoor*) was written by Verdi's great Neapolitan rival Saverio Mercadante at the height of his powers. Cammarano transposes the action to Scotland in 1570 and shuffles the characters among members of the court of the infant James VI: Gustave becomes the Regent Murray, Ankastrom the Duke of Hamilton and the conspirators are followers of the imprisoned Mary Stuart. Such nonsensical transformations were imposed upon dramatists by the authorities for different reasons in different states of the Italian peninsula. Italian censors were paranoically over-sensitive to any suggestion of political content in librettos. The mere mention of the name of the ruler would result in an instant demand for an alteration! In such a volatile political atmosphere, the idea of staging the assassination of a reigning monarch was inconceivable. It was finally agreed that the setting should be seventeenth-century Boston and that Gustave should become Riccardo, Conte di Warwich, the English Governor of the American colony!

While this historical absurdity was forced onto a reluctant and frequently protesting composer by the febrile politics of Risorgimento Italy, to maintain this setting today seems nonsensical — especially since the full dramatic force of the work depends on the royal status of the protagonist. If Riccardo were an ordinary citizen, then this would be a kitchen-sink tragedy, but as a king his personal weakness or virtue affects the well-being of the whole community. Verdi, deeply involved with the *Lear* project, fully understood the Shakespearean concept of the ruler as the source of all stability and success. The enormity of regicide as the destruction of social and universal order was intensely vivid to him and he wrote a work of regal stature. Moreover, he injected a powerful transfusion into the traditional operatic structure to do justice to the subject. The magnitude of this tragic treatment loses power in the emasculated context of Boston. The elements of vitality and humour (typified by Riccardo's *alter ego*, the page Oscar) have less coherence outside the functional brilliance of the court of an Enlightened despot. It is high time that we return to Sweden (even if we keep 'Riccardo' for the sake of euphony!) and restore Verdi's fully-fledged king.

This essay exploring the interaction of music and drama abandons the plot sequence in order to emphasise the special structural qualities of this distinctive, and frequently under-rated, opera.

Centre

The love duet in opera is mostly an opportunity for lyrical expressiveness and vocal display. It may release or concentrate dramatic energy but it is seldom used as the pivot of the dramatic process. Yet in *Un ballo in maschera* the love duet between Amelia and Riccardo is the irrevocable turning-point of the drama and is placed in the middle of the second Act — the centre of the work. It is more usual to find the dramatic crisis nearer the end of an opera, some two-thirds of the way through. We shall see that there is such a crux at that point when Renato ('Eri tu che macchiavi quell' anima' 'It was you who ensnared and defiled my love' [29]) makes the final decision to kill his master and friend. In carrying out his decision, he fulfils the prophecy made by Ulrica in the first Act (that Riccardo would be killed by a friend) and brings the drama to its tragic end. The prophecy and the fatal decision are counterparts of each other; these dramatically crucial elements are dependent on the encounter of the two lovers and are its structural supports.

Amelia, deeply tormented by her secret love for Riccardo, the ruler of the land and her husband's employer and friend, has taken the advice of the fortune-teller Ulrica that she can be cured of her affliction if she picks a magic herb under the gallows at midnight. This melodramatic gesture is a potent symbol: it identifies Amelia's psychological truths and dangers with an exceptionally delicate precision [20, 21]. Afraid and alone, Amelia is confronted by Riccardo — the very person she has come to exorcise. Her forbidden desire literally brings them together. Instead of finding release from her secret love, she is assaulted by his passionate protestations. Amelia digs deeply into her emotional resources [22], but she cannot sustain her resistance against the pressure of her own deeper desires and Riccardo's importunity. She finally succumbs, admits her love and falls into his arms.

For this major dramatic confrontation Verdi turns to the traditional formal pattern favoured by Rossini: the tripartite duet of three contrasted sections. If the first part was a tense dialogue between the couple then the second section might be a smooth, joint unity in which both voices would sing the same melodic material sensuously and tenderly. The third part might then be a

Kathleen Battle as Oscar and Luciano Pavarotti as Gustavus at San Francisco, 1982 (photo: Ira Novinski)

more energetic avowal, expression of danger — or whatever the dramatic situation called for. This pattern (with emotional and dramaturgical origins in the Baroque) allowed for sharp clarity within each section as well as emotional variety. Verdi knew its utility, but seldom used it directly, although a good example of the stock Rossinian approach (which also foretells a more intense treatment) is the grand duet of Carlo and Giovanna in *Giovanna d'Arco* (1843). In *Un ballo in maschera* he uses the pattern, but he makes very considerable changes to it.

Most extraordinary is the way that Verdi combines a great sense of expansiveness (appropriate to the timelessness of the lovers' emotions) with an immediate feeling of danger and pressing time — of a lurking menace which will, all too soon, overtake the lovers. The feeling of timelessness is communicated by a variety of nuance and musical treatment unparalleled in any earlier Verdi love duet. The start seems normal [23], but soon leads to a 'parlanto melodico' — a continuous orchestral melody partly doubled by the voices. The intensity rises and the music sways strongly from one texture and emotional area to another as Riccardo takes up Amelia's protests and, first gently, then passionately, intensifies his pleading. Amelia's resistance collapses ('Io son di lui, che daria la vita' 'I am the wife of a man who would die for you' [22]) in a succession of crotchet triplets. This triplet motion (within a C time signature, but reinforced by a stabbing

on each beat) echoes the second part of Ulrica's prophecy and its tonal centre; it finally [24] releases the dammed-up passion of the lovers in the cathartic *cabaletta* of the duet: 'O qual soave brivido' ('The sweetest glowing fire of love').

17

The duet is amazingly varied, but also remarkably compact, a combination which produces a sharp sense of concentration and intensity. As one element in an extended piece of musical architecture, it is preceded by a remarkable aria for Amelia [20], and followed by a harrowing encounter between the lovers (Amelia now veiled) and Renato — Riccardo's friend and Amelia's husband — when the latter warns that enemies are approaching. A formal trio ('Odi tu come fremono cupi' 'Do you hear, like a whispering in the dark' [25]) and the encounter with the conspirators screw up the tension. Only in the finale of the Act (when Riccardo has left) is the tension released in the ironic anti-climax of Renato's bitter discovery that he is escorting his own wife [26, 27]. Verdi treats the whole volatile complex in a single, unbroken span creating one of his largest formal constructs up to that time. He was not to exceed it until Act Four, scene one, of *Don Carlos* or the seamless expanse of the first Act of *Otello*.

First Pivot

The Prelude which opens the work is a subtle piece of musical craft. Based on thematic material from the opening scene [1], it allows the action revealed by the rising curtain to continue fluently — as though we had walked into a room where people were quietly conversing. This softly bustling scene evolves along divers threads and thus, almost casually, introduces the various characters and their temperamental features. Riccardo (who soon expresses his love for Amelia [3]), is generous (even sentimental) and more than a shade reckless as he dismisses Renato's warning of a conspiracy against his life. Renato, faithful and attentive, is also suspicious and passionate [4]. The page Oscar (a soprano in travesty who tops most ensembles) is a fun-loving youth — a sunny *alter ego* for Riccardo. Oscar represents that aspect of Riccardo's personality which lies beyond those restrictions imposed by his high office and the responsibilities which weigh it down. The comparison with *Lear* is telling: Shakespeare's king destroys his world through his selfishness. While Riccardo acknowledges the attraction of freedom from his status — he is often in disguise, flirting with danger — he does not have that blind self-ignorance which impels Shakespeare's old king to abdicate publicly. Both dramas examine the nature of kingship, and the human nobility of the ruler. Oscar tempts and assists Riccardo's desire for freedom [5, 6, 18, 32, 35] — until love and self-abandonment invoke Riccardo's self-destruction.

These deeper issues are only the wisps of a strange perfume in the air of a busy, brilliant first scene. Its direct purpose is to set the score and to introduce most of the protagonists, which Verdi achieves with newly-found contrapuntal brilliance and depth. The real activation of the drama (not unusually) is, however, postponed until scene two, which introduces the supernatural.

Three fierce diminished seventh chords played full force on the whole orchestra gradually embrace a dark C minor tonality. Ulrica's 'Re dell' abisso affrettati' ('Come, I invoke you Lucifer') [9] imprints a dark, ominous sound quite different from the luminous gaiety of the previous scene. Riccardo, generous and fair-minded, has received numerous complaints against the Negress Ulrica. He decides to investigate these personally and comes to her dwelling disguised as a fisherman. His jaunty appearance separates the two stanzas of her aria and almost evaporates the gloom, but his flippant request for a consultation is rebuffed. In the second stanza ('È lui; è lui che palpiti' 'The god! The god! I feel him now') Ulrica reinforces her sombre musings and

Act Two in Ebert's Glyndebourne production with Ljuba Welitsch as Amelia, Alda Noni as Oscar, and Paolo Silveri as Renato, at the 1949 Edinburgh Festival (photo: Angus McBean © Harvard Theatre Collection)

increases the sense of oppression. The coiling climax of her aria [10] reinforces our sense of her command in this mysterious world far more powerfully than the cheap theatrical trick of her disappearing in a puff of smoke.

The appearance of Silvano, a simple sailor, initiates the conflict between the human (even rationalist) world of Riccardo and the supernatural world of Ulrica. Silvano, three years in the service of Riccardo and having faced many hardships, asks for a fortune-telling ('Su, fatemi largo' 'Make way there, I'll ask her' [11]) and is told that fortune and promotion are soon to reward him. Riccardo, laughingly generous, promptly makes the promise 'true' by slipping an officer's commission into Silvano's pocket! All praise Ulrica's power when Silvano reaches into his pocket to pay the Negress and withdraws the commission — which (for our benefit) he reads to the admiring chorus. This trite conventional trick serves its purpose well enough.

The appearance of a servant from Amelia causes Ulrica to dismiss the bystanders. All leave, except Riccardo who has recognised the servant and hides in the shadows. Amelia's agitated entrance [12] immediately establishes her on the dark, disturbed side of the drama. Although she is the leading soprano and has her fair share of high notes, she seldom has the bright, shining brilliance normal to that part. Verdi sees her as tragic throughout and reserves sheer vocal brilliance for Oscar. Amelia's music is characterised by long, anguished phrases of very large span. She is deeply distressed and has sought this private consultation with Ulrica in a desperate effort to escape her secret love for Riccardo. Ulrica's calm, sensuously invasive rely, 'Della città all'

19

occaso' ('Out of the city, in the west') [13] gives us an early foretaste of Iago at his most seductive and suggests a fearful cure: the collection of a magic herb, at midnight under the gallows outside the town walls. This suggestion horrifies Amelia, which restores her frantic, disturbed music and finally releases itself in a soul-unwrapping prayer ('Consentimi, o Signore' 'I beg of you, dear Lord' [14]). The content and fervour of this plea is so burningly intense that both Ulrica and the hidden Riccardo join in and thus become co-plaintives of the prayer. All this is very much beyond the traditional two-movement cavatina which the Italian audience (and the singer!) would expect for the entrance of the *prima donna*. Mercadante provides the traditional treatment at the equivalent point in *Il reggente*. It has none of the overpowering intensity which Verdi injects into the situation by his expanded treatment.

Amelia leaves us impressed by the radiance of her personality; the crowd return. We know that Riccardo will again challenge the supernatural since out of love for Amelia he will follow her at midnight. Yet despite his ebullient subversion of magic forces, Riccardo exposes himself to Ulrica's powers. Parodying his fisherman's disguise he sings a folksy 6/8 *canzona* [15] and the chorus echo the refrain. Ulrica solemnly warns him not to mock ('Chi voi siate, l'audace parola può nel pianto prorompere un giorno' 'These are bold words to hear from a stranger, but be careful or you may regret them'), but he merely proffers Ulrica his hand and challenges her to foretell what his future holds. She reads his palm — and recoils in shock. Only under duress does she admit that she sees an immanent death — not on the field of battle (which Riccardo would welcome) but at the hand of a friend. After a pause, Riccardo laughs and proclaims his disbelief by launching the famous quintet with chorus 'È scherzo, od è follia' ('She may be mad, or does she joke') [16]. (This ensemble often gets the sobriquet 'laughing' because it has been traditional since Caruso's time for the tenor to interpolate real chuckles into the vocal line.) Well known and loved for its ebullience, this quintet is a bold invention which flashes between the dark and bright forces which drive and stress the drama. At the ensemble's end Riccardo demands to know the identity of his killer. Ulrica replies 'The man who is first to take you by the hand.' Riccardo challenges all those present to take his hand and give the lie to Ulrica's prophecy, but none will face the consequences. At that point Renato appears, concerned that his master is needlessly exposing himself to danger. At once, with great relief, he grasps his friend's proffered hand. The bystanders are shocked, but Riccardo is delighted with the joke, pointing out that Ulrica's powers did not even divine his true identity. He pays her handsomely and promises not to banish her. She, touched by his vivacity and generosity, warns him to be wary of traitors. With Silvano at their head the populace return and praise Riccardo [19]. We shall not meet Ulrica again. This may be extravagantly poor value from a manager's stand-point, but her appearance both dramatically and musically will haunt and control all that follows.

Second Pivot

In our century Béla Bartók often used symmetrical movement structures with a central peak (the so-called *arch* or *bridge* structures where movement I balances movement V; II mirrors IV). *Un ballo in maschera* comes very close to such a construction. Although Act Two is formally divided into four numbers, it is continuously composed so that the drama is forced towards an ineluctable result. Act One has two parts — the second of which (as we have seen)

The final scene in Ebert's Glyndebourne production with Ljuba Welitsch as Amelia, Mirto Picchi as Riccardo and Alda Noni as Oscar, 1949 (photo: Angus McBean © Harvard Theatre Collection)

establishes the dramatic conflicts. Act Three seems to break the symmetry with its three sections. One *could* argue that the second scene (during which Riccardo writes the letter which proves his generosity by commanding Amelia and Renato to continue their lives elsewhere) is no more than an opportunity for the tenor to have his conventional display piece or that it is a mechanical transition to enable the back-stage staff to change the scenery from the domestic action of Renato's study to the highly public ambience of the finale at the royal ball. No such sophistry is needed to point out that the start of Act Three perfectly balances the second part of Act One and that both symmetrically embrace the crucial second Act.

In the first scene of the last Act Renato, having been humiliated before the conspirators Samuel and Tom and having discovered what he believes to be his wife's infidelity, must face the apparent destruction of his life. Although Riccardo is his friend and his ruler, the suspected crime of adultery *must* be avenged. The opening instrumental music encompasses all Renato's fury and his dangerous strength. A passionate, bitter encounter with Amelia is no release: 'Sangue vuolsi e tu morrai' ('I'll have vengeance, you shall die') is Renato's demand (a phrase which Verdi insisted be added to the libretto: as so often, he demanded a cardinal phrase or image to gel the dramatic issue). As Renato draws his sword to complete the deed, Amelia falls to her knees and makes a last plea to be allowed to see their son once more ('Morrò ma prima in grazia' 'I'll die, but first I beg you' [28]). After coldly granting this request Renato is left alone and Verdi takes a leaf from Mercadante's *Il reggente* by giving his baritone a potent aria at this final dramatic turning point. This mighty taxing and emotionally supercharged aria [29] establishes Renato as the force of tragic retribution. His 'Eri tu' ('It was you') is addressed to the portrait of Riccardo for it is *his* blood which must flow to cleanse Renato's humour. The aria bursts abruptly on top of the word 'vendicator' ('I'll have revenge') at the close of the recitative. It totally transforms a conventional major-minor romance. The formal decasyllabic verse is treated very freely and flexibly; the music has no direct repetition yet it makes several oblique references to thematic elements from earlier scenes. It pulls and stretches across irregular phrase patterns which have the elasticity of recitative combined with the emotive power of heightened song. When the music finally turns to the relative major, as Renato takes leave of all the beauty in his life [30], there is no healing release: the dark, destructive issues are set hard. If Samuel and Tom are surprised that Renato should wish to join their conspiracy, we are not. Amelia is forced to draw their names from a vase to choose who shall have the honour of striking the fatal blow, Renato's joy and triumph that it should be he is unmitigated and (as he launches the militaristic trio of vengeance [31]) totally and horribly believable. Ulrica prophesied that Riccardo would be killed by a friend — the first to clasp his hand. Now Renato ensures that that dreadful forecast shall come true. Later, at the masked ball, Riccardo is secure in Amelia's love [37] and flaunts the danger which Ulrica prophesied and Renato warned against in the first Act. His courage is a public statement of his disbelief in superstition and of his confidence in the loyalty of his subjects.

Other Elements

Only twice, at each end of his working life, did Verdi write comedies. *Un giorno di regno* (*A King for a Day*) was a total disaster (although its complete failure is undeserved) — *Falstaff* needs no apology! This is not to say that Verdi's work is saturated tragedy. Tragedy gave him the scope for the kind of musico-dramatic intensity which he sought. Yet there are many examples of deftly sketched humorous characters and scenes in his work (e.g. Fra Melitone in *La forza del destino*). The dramatic structure of *Un ballo in maschera* is, as we have seen, predominantly concerned with the dark, doomed tragedy. The opera is, however, sprinkled with light and laughter. In its purest form this element is present through Oscar who shines brilliantly and sociably in Acts One and Three enjoying everyone and everything. He is not alone. There is the warm, direct humanity of the sailor Silvano who does not complain at the hard life that he leads and is openly grateful for the good fortune which comes to him. This life-enhancing quality is also the most endearing and well-projected trait of Riccardo's character. Even if he ultimately destroys himself by his scepticism and his passionate spontaneity, he communicates the sense not only of a king, but of a sparkling [16], generous [39], and laughter-loving man. His death leaves us diminished and drained, yet glad to have encountered such a vibrant character. No one can doubt Verdi's admiration for Shakespeare and — whether or not we restore Riccardo to his kingdom — Verdi has here created a role with the stature and the fatal, tragic flaw of a Shakespearean monarch.

The 'Laughing Chorus' in Contexts

Harold Powers

On May 12, 1858, from his Villa Sant' Agata in Busseto, Verdi wrote to his old friend Clarina Maffei in Milan:

> I got back from Naples ten or twelve days ago. (. . .) Now here I am, and after the turmoils of Naples, this profound peace is ever more dear to me. (. . .) Perhaps I'll go to Naples in the autumn, and to Rome for the Carnival season, if the Censorship there will allow the opera that was written for Naples; if not, so much the better, since that way I won't be writing anything, at least not for the coming Carnival season. From *Nabucco* onward I haven't had, one could say, an hour of peace. A sixteen-year sentence at hard labour! [*sedici anni di galera*][1]

It must be stressed that Verdi's 'anni di galera' really were sixteen; they did not end with the great successes of the early 1850s, as modern biographers often sentimentally imply. Indeed, the most unexpected shock he suffered during his 16-year sentence, and probably one of the worst, was the last. In the autumn of 1857 Verdi was told that the Bourbon censors in Naples had accepted a detailed prose summary of the opera in progress, an opera already adapted from its original subject of *Gustave III* in order to conform with what Verdi had been given to believe were their requirements. But when he finally submitted the versified libretto — now *Una vendetta in domino* — upon his arrival in Naples on January 14, 1858, to begin rehearsals, the censors rejected it; and not only had Verdi completed the composition before he left Busseto early in 1858, he had also well begun the orchestration in Genoa, while waiting out storms at sea *en route* to Naples. The shock at the rejection and the turmoil of attempts to adjust the libretto further were succeeded on February 17 by humiliation: without warning Verdi was handed a clumsy calque on *Una vendetta in domino*, called *Adelia degli Adimari*, approved for production only in that form. The turmoil continued in Verdi's refusal to allow his work to be produced with the substitute libretto, and in the lawsuit against him for so doing and his countersuit.

As soon as it was clear that his opera as set was not going to be approved, sometime in February 1858, he started thinking about a production in Rome, where an Italian play on the original *Gustave III* subject was running. Eventually Verdi and the Roman impresario Jacovacci mediated a compromise between the views of (this time) the poet Antonio Somma and the Papal censorship; a libretto very close to the one Verdi had already set for Naples was approved for printing, and Verdi supervised its production as *Un ballo in maschera* in February 1859. And, as he had intimated to Clarina Maffei, he had indeed spent six weeks in Naples the previous autumn preparing the Neapolitan première of *Simon Boccanegra*, as part of the out-of-court settlement of suit and countersuit.

Verdi's worst trials during his 'anni di galera' were his bouts with pre-1861 censorships, beginning with *Ernani*, reaching a first climax with *Stiffelio* and *Rigoletto*, and culminating in his Neapolitan imbroglio, just three years before the disappearance of the Kingdom of the Two Sicilies into the Kingdom of Italy. These battles were not edifying for Verdi nor, on the whole, are they for

23

us, critically speaking. But the *Ballo* case is different, for Verdi's detailed comments on *Adelia degli Adimari*, intended to justify in court his refusal to allow the music for *Una vendetta in domino* to be performed with that libretto, point up many salient features of his conception of *Un ballo in maschera* as we now know it.[2]

His voluminous correspondence in general, and with his librettists in particular, is the most important material we have on the musical dramaturgy of Italian opera. In the correspondence with Somma may be either found or inferred many of the most important premises regarding the relationship of verse metre and stanza design with musical phrase and period structure.[3] Somma was a poet of some standing in his time, unlike Piave for instance; yet — unlike Cammarano, Ghislanzoni, and Boito — Somma had little notion of the special traditions and requirements of poetry for the musical theatre. Verdi instructed him, tactfully but often in detail, during their work on *Re Lear* and *Gustave III/Una vendetta in domino/Un ballo in maschera*. He needed to, for an Italian opera is not a sung verse play in Italian amplified by continuous background music. When Verdi wrote on September 19, 1857 to Vincenzo Torelli, the Neapolitan impresario with whom he had contracted for the ensuing Carnival season, of a certain Spanish play, that 'in making the outline [*schizzo*] for reducing it to *proporzioni musicabili*' he had found it unsuitable, it was not merely shortening it for the slower pace of music that he will have had in mind.[4] Verdi went on to report to Torelli that he was now 'reducing a French *dramma*, *Gustavo III di Svezia*, a libretto of Scribe's, and produced at the Opéra more than twenty years ago.'

For Verdi three things were essential for a *dramma* to be *musicabile*: a palpable ambience, striking characters, and above all, strong situations.[5] Scribe's *Gustave* had all three in abundance. Indeed, it had already shown itself to be *musicabile*, not only in the original French for Auber in 1833 but also in bowdlerized Italian guises in Salvadore Cammarano's libretto *Il reggente* for Saverio Mercadante's music (Turin 1842/3), and Gaetano Rossi's libretto *Clemenza di Valois* for music by Vincenzo Gabussi (Venice 1840/1).[6]

The Atmosphere
When the Neapolitan Bourbon censors in 1857 found assassination and superstition in the Swedish royal court of 1792 too close for comfort, Somma suggested

> it wouldn't be bad to put it in Pomerania (. . .) an independent duchy in the 12th century (. . .) a time in which superstitions must have embraced a large proportion of classes (. . .) and we could make up a Duke at our pleasure (. . .) With the King changed to a Duke, our Ankarstroem would become a Count, and Stockholm, Stettin (. . .) (November 19, 1857)

Verdi reacted doubtfully, pointing out what was essential regarding the locale, the general ambience and the two light-hearted characters personifying that ambience.

> It just seems to me that the 12th century is too far off for our *Gustavo*. It is a time so rough, so brutal, especially in those countries, that it seems to me a serious contradiction to put in characters of a French cut like Gustavo and Oscar, and a *dramma* so brilliant and formed according to

Eva Turner as Amelia and Arthur Fear as Renato at Covent Garden, 1935 (photo: Royal Opera House Archives)

the customs of our time. One would need to find a Princeling, a Duke, a Devil, by all means to the North, that would have seen something of the world and smelt something of the odour of the court of Louis XIV. When the *dramma* is finished, you can think about it at your leisure. (November 26, 1857)

Earlier the same autumn he had made the same point to Torelli.

I've sent the poet your letter and I think it will not be difficult to transfer the setting elsewhere and change the names, but now that the poet is panting to go [*in lena*], it's better to finish the *dramma*, then we'll think about changing the subject. (October 14, 1857)

Obviously any locale would do for Verdi, so long as it did not contradict the ambience and character types suitable to what was important to him, the *dramma*. It was important only that the principal character be an absolute ruler, at least locally, and that he be an aristocrat of liberal views, scornful of superstition, personally both good-humoured and passionate, a man of the world living in a world where frivolities like masquerades were conceivable. A remote yet prosperous British colony during the Restoration could have seemed just the thing; given the average level of European cognizance of American history in the mid-19th century, it is no surprise that neither Verdi nor Somma knew that New England in the time of Charles II was not an overseas replication of the Restoration court but, so to speak, a reaction against it.

In one of his objections to *Adelia degli Adimari* Verdi set the sophisticated ambience of the court and the careless generosity of its central character against the strongly contrasted foreground of the *dramma* itself, referring to

> that certain *je ne sais quoi* of brilliance and chivalry, that certain aura of gaiety that was running through the whole action and making a beautiful contrast and was like light in the shadows of the tragic points of the *dramma*.[7]

In Scribe's *Gustave*, as in the Italian derivatives (of which Somma's and Verdi's is much the closest to the original), a series of striking situations crystallize out of this bipolar contrast of light and shadows, this *chiaroscuro* of atmosphere and character, making possible a number of those musical ensembles, *a tutta ribalta* (everybody up to the footlights), those time-stopping moments of contrasted individual and collective inner reactions (where the characters sing their hearts out), that are the unique glory of opera in the Great Tradition. The most striking instance is the central Finale, in which the catastrophe is precipitated, and which concludes Act Three of Auber's *Gustave* and Act Two of the Italian operatic versions.

The final 'action' of this Act is prepared by three 'actions', each formally marked by the entrance of a character. There are two 'moments of truth' — one private and one public. The first action, leading to the private moment of truth in the second, is simple; the third action, leading to the public moment of truth in the fourth, is complex. Table I outlines the four actions.

Most of the differences between the four versions in the second half of the Act are trivial but three are significant. First, in *Il reggente* action 4.c was eliminated: this is linked to the reaction of the conspirators in the ensemble. Secondly, in *Ballo* when action 4.e resumes, the conspirators make ready to depart *after* the husband has addressed them, rather than before; this is connected with Verdi's manipulations of central Finale conventions.

Thirdly, the elimination from *Il reggente* of action 4.c influenced the staging of action 4.d in *Ballo*. In *Gustave* (and in *Ballo*), the scene description for the Act concludes 'several parts of it are lit up by the moon'; that is, the stage is partly illuminated and partly in shadow. In *Clemenza di Valois*, to the contrary, the *chiaroscuro* is temporal, 'the moon hidden among the clouds shows itself sometimes'; that is, the stage is bright at some times and dark at others. But for Rossi as for Scribe the moon was merely part of the midnight atmosphere, and at the public moment of truth the lady's face was revealed by torches brought forward by conspirators just as it had been in *Gustave*.

Cammarano on the other hand, having eliminated action 4.c, which includes not only the bantering but also the bringing forward of torches, needed another way to illuminate the lady's face. He may have taken the hint from Rossi's purely atmospheric set description, but his own is already much more vivid: 'the sky is covered with thick clouds, which — moved by the wind — now reveal, now hide, the moon'. The Acts of *Il reggente*, moreover, have titles, as was Cammarano's practice, and Act Two is called *La dama velata* ('the veiled lady').

As the lady intervenes and her veil falls, Cammarano's direction reads

> at that very moment the thick cloud cover that was hiding the moon disperses, and it appears in all its splendour

so that her face is illuminated by moonlight rather than by torches. And since

Table I: The four actions of the central Act of *Gustave III/
Clemenza di Valois/Il reggente/Un ballo in maschera*

Setting: midnight; a fearful spot outside the city, associated with executed criminals; the scene is partially/sometimes lit by the moon. In *Gustave* and *Ballo*, the setting is the execution ground, while in *Clemenza* and *Il reggente* it is the place where criminals are buried.

Action 1. The lady enters, wearing a veil; her face is sometimes visible, sometimes hidden. She is terrified but determined to pluck the herb that will extinguish her passion for the ruler.

Action 2. The ruler enters.
    a.   i)   He declares his love;
         ii)   he persists, she resists.
    b.   i)   He forces her to confess her love (**the private moment of truth**);
         ii)   they hover on the verge of an affair.
    c.   they hear someone coming.

Action 3. The ruler's best friend enters.
    a.   He warns the ruler that conspirators approach to assassinate him, identifying him by the veiled lady with him.
    b.   He wants the ruler to escape, leaving the lady behind.
    c.   The ruler refuses to abandon the lady.
    d.   The lady threatens to unveil if the ruler will not save himself.
    e.   The ruler makes his friend swear to escort the veiled lady to safety.
    f.   The three hear the footsteps of the conspirators.
    g.   The ruler departs.

Action 4. The conspirators enter.
    a.   The lady is fearful; the ruler's friend reassures her.
    b.   i)   the conspirators enter menacingly;
         ii)   believing the man to be the ruler,
         iii)   they prepare to attack.
    c.   i)   He challenges them;
         ii)   seeing that it is only the ruler's friend, the conspirators' mood changes from bloodthirsty to bantering, some come forward with torches, and they demand to see the veiled beauty with whom (they suppose) he has an assignation;
         iii)   he draws his sword to defend her anonymity, and they prepare to attack.
    d.   i)   The veiled lady intervenes;
         ii)   her veil accidentally falls and all see that she is the wife of the friend himself (**the public moment of truth**).
    –   All react according to their contrasted feelings: **ensemble 'a tutta ribalta'**.
    e.   i)   The conspirators make ready to leave;
         ii)   the ruler's friend makes an appointment to meet them;
         iii)   he reminds the lady that he has sworn to escort her back to safety.
    –   All react to the further developments.

---

the Italian pronoun 'essa' can equally well mean 'she' or 'it', an intentional ambiguity in Cammarano's stage direction as well as his title for the Act can hardly be doubted: 'the veiled lady' is both the moon and the heroine. Now in Somma's first version (November 15, 1857), there is no mention of the moon at the moment of truth but, during his subsequent revisions, stage directions for the gradual unveiling of the moon within the Act appear and grow ever closer to the version we know now, which culminates in language so close to Cammarano's as to make the inference that Somma borrowed from Cammarano undeniable. This is confirmed by Somma's failure to eliminate directions left over from earlier drafts. For instance, during action 4.c conspirators still come forward, as in *Gustave*, with torches that have become superfluous, and even distracting, for the use of the moon to illuminate the lady is a show-stopping moment that no producer should pass by.

And stop the show it does, for this enlightenment, this public moment of truth, is the launching pad for that musical ensemble 'a tutta ribalta'. This grand *tableau vivant* of outraged husband, of unveiled lady, and of thwarted conspirators carries the musical weight of one of the two musical numbers that this Act has in common in all four operas, the other being the 'private moment of truth', the duet when the lady confesses her love. In *Gustave* and *Ballo*, the duet and the finale are the second and fourth numbers in an aria-duet-trio-finale sequence characteristic of both French Grand Opéra and Italian Romantic *melodramma*. Within musical numbers, however, French and Italian conventions differed, and the dynamic of individual numbers in *Ballo* is more profitably compared with the other Italian versions.

The unveiling
All the Italian versions have a few lines of recitative after the duet when the lovers hear someone approaching (action 2.c) and then, with the entry of the ruler's friend, action 3 begins.

Il reggente is very condensed. From action 2.c all the way through action 3 and into action 4.a, everything is in recitative verse — *versi sciolti* — and recitative musical texture: there is no formal trio between the duet and the finale. The poetry changes to the regular line length and rhyme of lyric verse (*versi lirici*) for conspirators (action 4.b), with a quatrain of *settenari*. Even so, the first two lines are set in recitative; the strict musical time, *tempo giusto*, that is normally used for lyric verse begins only with the third line, which is followed by an orchestral *crescendo* and a choral outburst for the fourth line 'Mora l'indegno, mora!' [let the wretch die!], as the conspirators launch their attack. Action 4.d follows with a second quatrain of *settenario* verse as the lady intervenes and she is recognized. The action stops: the music for the recognition, as in *Ballo*, continues in *tempo giusto*, in a characteristic unwinding *decrescendo* for the stunned reaction of all parties, modulating towards the tonality of the ensemble to follow.

If in *Il reggente* the treatment is the most direct, in *Clemenza di Valois* it is the most conventional (see Table II). As in *Gustave*, action 3 is a trio, here retailored for the standard Italian succession of movements in ensembles, with a preliminary *scena* in recitative verse and music, followed by four movements in lyric verse and *tempo giusto*. In this standard sequence, the first and third ('kinetic') sections move the action forward: the melodic continuity is in the orchestra with versified dialogue set over it (*parlante*), either with the singers declaiming on chord tones (*armonico*) or doubling the orchestral melody here

28

Table II: Rossi/Gabussi, *Clemenza di Valois* Act Two, trio
An example of a standard Italian sequence of movements for a trio.

Scena: recitative verse (*versi sciolti*) and musical texture: actions 2.c and 3.a.

Tempo d'attacco (kinetic): *ottonario* lyric verse; *moderato* 4/4, f minor/F Major, then *più mosso* and modulations: for actions 3.b-c.

Adagio (static): one [6+4 line] stanza of *settenario* lyric verse for each character; *adagio*, 2/4, Db Major. There is no action.

Tempo di mezzo (kinetic): *settenario* lyric verse; *agitato assai*, 4/4 modulating: actions 3.d-e.

Stretta (static): one 8-line stanza of two quatrains of *ottonario* lyric verse for each character; *allegro*, 4/4, F Major: action 3.f.

---

and there (*melodico*). The second and fourth movements are 'static': the characters' reactions are in lyric verse stanzas that are vehicles for expressive music, with the melodic continuity in the voice parts and the orchestra accompanying.

The corresponding number in *Ballo* has two lyric movements rather than four. Action 3.f gives one stanza of lyric verse to each character, a pair of quatrains of *decasillabo* (ten syllable lines), and is composed as formal music.[8] A single kinetic movement sets a string of *ottonario* (eight syllable lines) verses that covers actions 3.a-e. This piece is outlined in Table III.

It will be evident that changes from one verse metre to another are correlated with changes from one musical movement to another. There are parallel structures of drama, versification, and musical design in all three operas. The drama turns on action 4.d, the public moment of truth, which comes at the end of a long preparatory movement in two cases, and is heavily marked musically in all three: in *Clemenza di Valois* by an abrupt change of tempo and key; in *Il reggente* by a sudden shift in the harmony followed by a

Table III: Somma/Verdi, *Un ballo in maschera*, Act Two, trio
(No. 5 in Verdi's autograph but unnumbered in the printed score)

Scena: 3 lines of *versi sciolti* recitative: action 2.c.

Quasi tempo d'attacco: 28 lines of *senario doppio* lyric verse, for actions 3.a-e (dialogue except for bars 43-54);

Allegro mosso, 4/4, F Major (*parlante armonico/melodico*)
    a. bars 1-20, F Major: principal subject, * lyrical extension, and *cadence, for action 3.a
    b. bars 21-33, f minor → Db Major → bb minor: development of the principal subject, for action 3.b
    c. bars 34-58, changing harmonies over a dominant pedal of F Major: *lyrical return, for action 3.c
    d. bars 39-42, F Major: principal subject and *cadence, for action 3.d
    — bars 43-54, F Major: *lyrical conclusion, no action
    e. bars 55-73, modulating: declamatory, for action 3.e

---

* The two passages designated 'cadence' are similar and parallel, as are the two passages characterized as 'lyrical extension' and 'lyrical return'. Amelia's 'lyrical conclusion' combines musical gestures reminiscent of both.

---

long *decrescendo* that modulates sequentially as it goes, slowing and finally stopping the action, in a fashion common in the genre; in much the same way in *Ballo*, by a sudden harmonic shift (which Verdi finalized only late in the compositional process) followed by a long *decrescendo*, and with the tempo redoubled.

All three finales rest on the ensembles *a tutta ribalta*. There is always a complete change of poetic design, verse metre, and tempo at this point in a big central Finale. After the slow movements there is always a change back to a faster tempo for a *tempo di mezzo* and, though the verse metre does not always change, the verses are once again broken for dialogue. Going into the static *stretta* the music sometimes continues the pacing of the *tempo di mezzo* (as in *Clemenza di Valois*), but the verse structure is much more regular.

In *Ballo* the verse metre changes for the resumption of action after the slow ensemble and, though the background tempo does not change, the musical textures and rhythms for the new verses differ violently from those of the *quinari doppi* (two-part five syllable lines); but those new verses and music are interspersed with reversions to the preceding text and music. The anomalous absence in *Ballo* of new verse or music for a *stretta* to finish the conventional sequence is discussed below.

Gaetano Rossi's text is the closest to Scribe's and Cammarano differs the most radically. But both Rossi and Cammarano followed the original design after the *coup de théâtre* of action 4.d. The French convention called for the ensembles to be treated as a refrain framing intermediate action, with the same or nearly the same text, and the same or nearly the same music, and so it was in *Gustave*. The Italian convention was more dynamic: the action following the first (slow) ensemble should change things enough to provoke at least somewhat different reactions to allow for a different kind of ensemble, a *stretta*, to follow. Scribe's plot made that awkward: neither the husband's nor the wife's state of mind is altered in the action after the first ensemble, and the conspirators move at best from one kind of puzzlement to another. And indeed, though Rossi's ensemble texts are different in form, as required by the Italian convention, the changes in substance are slight and the conspirators are still amused. But all traces of mockery or irony in Scribe's words or actions were finessed by Cammarano from the start. In the first ensemble of *Il reggente* the husband leads off but the conspirators catch on right away: noting that the husband is red with fury while the wife is deathly pale, they see that friendship has given way to rage; by the second ensemble husband and conspirators are at one and they sing the same words; only the lady has a separate text.

The composition

Somma's first two surviving letters to Verdi regarding what became *Un ballo in maschera* were a request for guidance and an acknowledgement of it.

> [October 13, 1857] I agree to versify *Gustavo III di Svezia* according to the *versione* that you are hastening to send me. Besides the scenario [*sceneggiatura*] with which you are going to favour me, it will be useful for the musical rhythm that you note for me in the margin the form of the stanzas, the verse metre, and the number of lines to each stanza, so

Maria Callas in costume for Amelia with Ghiringhelli, general director of La Scala, Milan, in 1957 (photo: Popperfoto)

that I can offer you suitable poetry. To this end, please be profuse in your advice.

[October 24, 1857] I have received your last, with the *versione* and the original, and I have immediately set to work.[9]

Though the annotated *versione* that Verdi sent Somma has not turned up, we may be sure that it was a detailed summary in prose.[10] And we may infer that it specified the then unusual design for the Act Two finale: a string of verses for action leading up to a set of stanzas for an ensemble, and, after the ensemble, another string of verses for action leading not to a second set of stanzas for a *stretta* but rather to a curtain. Somma's first draft, sent on November 15, has that design, and it differs from the final version only in that the stanzas for the ensemble had to be changed from *endecasillabi lirici* — eleven syllables — ('Qui nel cor della notte e colla sposa/Cerca dolcezze il Duca innamorato!') to *quinari doppi* ('Ve' se di notte qui colla sposa/L'inamorato conte riposa'). Eventually there were four stanzas rather than three.

We may also be sure not only that Verdi deliberately set up the scenario to abort a *stretta* but also that he was planning from the outset to mingle portions of verse and music from the static ensemble movement with the kinetic verses and music for the action that follows. Since the intermingled text is not new there is no evidence in a libretto for such a plan, but Verdi had tried out the device once before. His correspondence with Cammarano regarding the Act One finale of *Luisa Miller* documents his intent to eschew a *stretta* while keeping the first three movements of the standard sequence (Table II).[11] Similarly in *Il trovatore* he had discarded a *stretta*, provided by Cammarano for the Act Two finale, and the Act concludes with *decasillabi* for an action movement, as in Luisa Miller, but just before the end they are interrupted by two lines from the preceding static ensemble.[12]

Once noted, it is not difficult to perceive the weaving of the 'laughing chorus' into the concluding action as a musico-dramatic technique for central finales without a *stretta* that Verdi had initiated with *Luisa Miller* and further developed in *Il trovatore*. It is evident from his correspondence that he worked over this finale, though since the continuity draft is unavailable, and no sketches for the finale are known to have survived, we cannot confirm the stages of the work with complete confidence.[13] But if it can be shown that a number was put together piecemeal, this is likely to bear on the final relationship of parts to whole, and can help account for the effect in the theatre. There are a few obvious discrepancies between the libretto and the music for the central Finale that make an easy opening for this discussion, and there is a firm base for partial reconstruction in Somma's drafts and Verdi's responses. There are also tantalizing scratchouts, crossouts and pasted-in pages in the autograph orchestral score. Table IV outlines the completed form of the ensemble.

Verdi's ensemble has four stanzas where the other Italian versions have three. In addition to the furious husband and anguished wife, Verdi wanted to distinguish two aspects of the conspirators' amused reaction. In one of his comments on *Adelia degli Adimari* he pointed out that

> in my *dramma* the irony of these two personages [the two chief conspirators], the cheerfulness of the Chorus [the rest of the conspirators], the desolation of the lady, the rage of the husband, formed a magnificent musical *tableau* [quadro].[14]

The distinction between ironic sarcasm and cheerful gossip is beautifully made in Verdi's opening music. An attentive reader of the libretto (page 77) will notice that the first of the four stanzas for the ensemble appears to be an anomalous sestet, with the two gossipy 'E che baccano' lines at the end, lines that seem rather more appropriate to 'the cheerfulness of the Chorus [the rest of the conspirators]', whose quatrain they complete, than to 'the irony of these

Table IV: The 'laughing chorus' from *Un ballo in maschera*.
Poetic metres are *quinario doppio* (stanzas) and *ottonario*
Andante mosso quasi Allegretto, 4/4

characters[1]	poetry[2]	no. bars[3]	tonality[4]	content[5]
Sam	stanza 1	10 ⎤ ⎫		
Sam/Tom	stanza 2.bCD	6 ⎦ ⎬ B♭		maggiore
Ren/Am	⎧ stanzas 4.AB/3.AB	4	g > d ⎫	minore
	⎨ stanzas 4.CD/3.CD	4	d > F ⎬	
	⎩ stanzas 4.D/3.D	2	F ⎭	
⎧ Sam/Tom	stanza 2.bCD	⎫		
⎨ Ren/Am	stanzas 4.CD/3.CD	⎬ 4 ⎫	B♭	tutti
⎩ + chorus	stanza 2.bCD	2 ⎭ ⎬		
⎧ Am/Ren	stanzas 3.abCD/4	⎫		
⎩ Sam/Tom/Chorus	stanza 2.AbCD	⎬ 8 ⎤		
⎧ Am/Ren	stanzas 3.abCD/4	⎫ ⎬ B♭		ritornello
⎩ Sam/Tom/Chorus	stanza 2.AbCD	⎬ 8 ⎦		
⎧ Sam/Tom				
⎩ chorus	⎬ stanza 2.CD	6	g ~ B♭	coda
Ren/Sam/Tom	ottonari (6)	6	mods > D♭	4.e.ii
Sam/Tom/chorus	ottonari (4)	6	b♭	4.e.i.
	stanza 2.AbCD	10	B♭	ripresa
⎧ Ren/Am	ottonari (4)	⎫		
⎩ chorus	stanza 2.b	⎬ 4	b♭/B♭	4.e.iii
Sam/Tom/chorus	stanza 2.bCD	6	B♭	ripresa
[orchestra]	— —	4	B♭	[curtain]

1. Curly brackets pointing right and the obliques indicate simultaneity.

2. The stanzas of *quinario doppio* (ie two-part five syllable lines) show the peculiarities of metrical counting in Italian convention. The number of syllables could be truncated to four (e.g. 'ah! ah! ah! ah!) or extended to six (a *sdrucciolo*: 'Piacevolissima'), so that the whole *quinario doppio* might be anything from eight to twelve syllables.

1. **SAM/TOM**	2. **CHORUS**
A. Ve' se di notte qui colla sposa	A. Ve', la tragedia mutò in commedia
B. L'innamorato campion si posa	B. Piacevolissima, ah! ah! ah! ah!
C. E come al raggio lunar del miele	C. E che baccano sul caso strano
D. Sulle rugiade corcar si sa!	D. E che commenti per la città!
3. **AMELIA**	4. **RENATO**
A. A chi nel mondo crudel più mai,	A. Così mi paga se l'ho salvato!
B. Misera Amelia, ti volgerai?	B. Ei m'ha la donna contaminato!
C. La tua spregiata lacrima, quale,	C. Per lui non posso levar la fronte,
D. Qual man pietosa rasciugherà?	D. Sbranato il core per sempre m'ha!

Lower-case means only *half* a line, and 2b means 'ah! ah! ah!' (three laughs). The number of lines in each *ottonario* verse is given in parentheses.

3. Vertical square brackets indicate the two stretches overlap.

4. Upper-case tonality letters denote Major keys. Lower-case tonality letters denote minor keys. > = moves to; mods = modulations. ~ = alternates with

5. The Italian words are musical terms for passages in the static movement.

two personages [the two chief conspirators]'. And there is an egregious discrepancy between the second line of the chorus's stanza and the music of the ensemble. The first *quinario* of the *quinario doppio*, 'piacevolissima', is never sung at all, and the laughs seemingly called for in the second *quinario* 'ah! ah! ah! ah!' come not in fours but in those sets of three noted earlier, sung as three equally spaced afterbeats after the downbeat in the orchestral bass.[15]

This is not random omission and selection; Verdi was very serious about his texts. The discrepancies arose because he had composed the musical units before receiving the four equal quatrains as they appear in *Adelia degli Adimari* and in the original printed libretto.

Somma sent Verdi his second version of the ensemble in *quinari doppi* early in December 1857, so that by the time he arrived at Sant'Agata later in the month, quatrains of *quinario doppio* — with all their possibilities and their limitations for musical rhythm, phrase, and period shaping — had been settled as the metre. During the visit they agreed that the chorus too should have a couple of lines, which would appear in the libretto in the usual place, after the three stanzas for the principles; after his return to Venice Somma sent Verdi two pairs of lines of which both as a quatrain or either as a pair by itself might be useful.

SOME OF THE PARTISANS

See, this is splendid, a funny story,	Ve' se l'è bella, la storiella,
All of the court will have a laugh.	Tutta la corte ne riderà.

OTHERS

A piece of gossip to spread around,	E che baccano sul caso strano
A charming story for all the town.	E che commenti per la città.

Verdi also thought a separate quatrain for the chorus appropriate, but he didn't want to have the chorus text shown after all the stanzas for the principals because the two lines were to be sung immediately after the first stanza. And though he asked for a quatrain for the chorus, the fragment that he sent, seemingly as a sample of the 'almost comic tone' he wanted, was more than just a sample. Verdi stated that he 'must make heard right after the stanza of *Ermanno* and *Manuel* [*i.e.* Samuel and Tom] two lines for the chorus', and that he had 'already done the music after the two stanzas for the husband and wife'. That being so, the fragment

Ah! ah! ah!	Ah! ah! ah!
What a story to tell	Vaga storiella — da raccontare
Tomorrow at court — and in town.	Domani a corte — ed in città.

may have served him temporarily as text for the music he had written for the *tutti* and *ritornello* ('after the two stanzas for the husband and wife'), and for the music he planned after the opening quatrain. Composing to his own text in the metre of verse still awaited from his poet was not unusual for Verdi. He had probably also composed the *minore*, the stanzas for Renato and Amelia.

The opening quatrain for Samuel and Tom was probably composed first; then the *minore*, the *tutti*, and the first statement of the *ritornello*, all using the 'vaga storiella' text Verdi sent as a 'sample' to Somma. Then when Verdi received the 'E che baccano' text, he substituted those words for the 'vaga storiella' text in the music that he had 'already done . . . after the two stanzas for the husband and wife', and after the opening quatrain.

Somma's final version reached Verdi in Genoa, or even in Naples, and he

Ragnar Ulfung as Gustavus and Birgit Nordin as his page at the Royal Opera, Stockholm, in 1958 (photo: Enar Merkel Rydberg)

used the first line (presumably instead of 'vaga storiella') for the non-laughing chorus parts in the *ritornello* and in the first *ripresa*, the only places where it appears. Thus the famous phrase 'Ve' la tragedia — mutò in commedia', rightly noted by almost all critics as the poetic key to the ironic contrast in the characters' perceptions of this doubly ambivalent situation, actually appears only twice: buried in the supporting choral mass of the *ritornello* — always the grandest part of an ensemble *a tutta ribalta*, with everyone singing full voice and no words heard — and sung once almost at the end, not by the chorus but by the chief conspirators.

As for the second line of Somma's last-minute choral stanza, Verdi never used it at all. The second *quinario* of the *quinario doppio* has four laughs, 'ah! ah! ah! ah!', but Verdi had long since settled his laughing in three sets of snickers each, the 'ah! ah! ah!' of the 'sample' sent to Somma in the last days of 1857. The first *quinario* 'piacevolissima' is *sdrucciolo* — slithered out by making the syllable-counting final trochee into a dactyl — and it is the only unambiguous and unelidable *sdrucciolo* in the entire text. Given the musical rhythms already composed, it was unusable.

The chiaroscuro
In the Act Two finale of *Un ballo in maschera* the '*parola scenica*' — Verdi's expression for that word or phrase that freezes the action and launches an ensemble — is Renato's cry 'Che! Amelia!' after the lady's veil falls: it leaps a tritone from c' to f#'. The harmony reached at the baritone's high note is a dominant in the key of g minor, prolonged in a 16-bar *diminuendo* winding down over a dominant pedal D, followed by a general pause. But the tension of that protracted irresolution is not resolved at the start of the ensemble: it is burst like a balloon, by a half-bar orchestral vamp in Bb Major, and by the skippy *staccato-legato* sarcasm of Samuel's 'Ve' se la notte — qui colla sposa'. The striking harmonic aspect of this collapse into Bb was an afterthought! The

original preparation for the B♭ Major was a predictable 16-bar winding down in its own dominant. The f#′ that Verdi entered for Renato's cry was not at first a sharp, and the orchestral bass note that was later replaced by D was also a simple F; scratched-out notes in the first violin part (the other instruments were entered after the change of harmony had been made) also originally prolonged the dominant in B♭ Major/minor.

This last-minute change may have been prompted by the dark side of the *chiaroscuro*. The contrast of the two harmonies does garishly limelight the artful vulgarity of the Major at the immediate juxtaposition, but the frustrated g minor does appear, delayed until the start of the lovers' impassioned music. There is a comparable contrast in the rhythmic pacing of the *quinari* in the two sections.

The elemental contrast of Major with minor is one obvious musical demonstration of Verdi's concern for the 'beautiful contrast . . . like light in the shadows of the tragic', though in the Act Two Finale it is light, if here of a rather spooky sort, that predominates — moonlight on the stage, Major in the music, ironic cheer in the text — while fury and anguish and the minor mode lurk and threaten in the shadows. In other ensemble movements, the contrast of light and shadow is also embodied in the Major/minor contrast, sometimes accompanied with contrasts in rhythm and pacing, sometimes not. In three of them moreover — movements like the 'laughing chorus' that immediately precede a curtain or follow a *coup de théâtre* — the tonality is also B♭ Major and minor.

The most straightforward is the quintet that closes Act Three, scene one. No sooner has Amelia drawn the murderer's name from the urn than Oscar enters with an invitation to a masked ball; the two sopranos make the Major-minor contrast at the onset. Their eight-bar melodies are identical but for the

Act Three at Sadler's Wells, 1965, with Elizabeth Fretwell, Stafford Dean, Robert Bickerstaffe, Kelvin Jones and Diane Todd (photo: Houston Rogers)

mode, like the positive and negative of photograph. When Samuel and Tom enter, they sing the old title of the opera 'una vendetta in domino' in b♭ minor, and so it continues in minor and Major to the end. The final ensemble after the assassination is also based on this modal contrast, and this time it is b♭ minor that predominates. The turns to B♭ Major are for Riccardo's dying assurances to Renato of Amelia's unsullied honour, and for his farewells.

The most interesting Major-minor shadings and modulations occur, however, in the 'laughing tenor' quintet at the end of Act One (strictly speaking, the static ensemble *a tutta ribalta* of a standard four-movement finale in which the final chorus functions as a *stretta*). The *coup de théâtre* is Ulrica's prophecy that Riccardo will die by the hand of a friend. The *parola scenica* is her 'No . . . per man d'un amico', followed in the usual way by a *fortissimo* shout and a mass winding down ending softly with 'Quale orror!' An astonishing transformation follows from ominous triplets in the timpani to light-hearted octave-skipping triplets in the woodwinds. It moves from darkness to light like the more abrupt transition into the ensemble of the Act Two finale, except that the light here is not grimly garish but genuinely gay — at least at the start.

In this quintet the initial Major/minor contrasts are accompanied by contrasts in pace and texture as well. Riccardo leads in B♭ Major, in the famous 'È scherzo od è follia' with its dancing dotted smallscale skips hopping both upward and downward; Ulrica responds in b♭ minor with a smoother line in quavers, rising in consecutive steps and falling in consecutive thirds, pointedly asking Samuel and Tom why her words seem to make them nervous;

they speak fearfully to one another of her seeming second sight, using a stop-and-go motif in semiquavers that seems slightly ridiculous at this first appearance in F Major. Then comes a magical one-bar modulation, in two diverging unaccompanied melodic lines, to the next key for the next passage. That passage is the *ritornello*, twice four bars of heartrendingly lovely D*b* Major, soft but full, with everybody on stage participating, and the soaring soprano above it all. It is Major, but it is the relative Major belonging to b*b* minor, and the turn that way has the same poignant effect as the turn to G*b* Major in the b*b* minor ensemble at the opera's end.

And for his *ritornello* Verdi made a virtue of an unconventional feature of the plot. In Scribe's design — which Verdi followed — the *prima donna* appears in only one number in the first two Acts (*i.e.* a rather long Act One in the Italian versions) and this is not it. The only character available here to carry the climactic high *legato* lyric line is Oscar, the frivolous page. But Oscar is not reacting frivolously at this moment; he is superstitious, and Ulrica's prophecy arouses both wonder and alarm in him as well as in the chorus, whose words he shares.

Is this how fate is ordered	E tal fia dunque il fato,
that he must now be murdered?	Ch'ei cade assassinato?
I cannot bear to think of it;	Al sol pensarci, l'anima
I shudder in my heart.	Abbrividendo va.

In order for Oscar to fulfil the musical requirements of the climactic *ritornello*, Verdi presumed a strain of pathos in this text. Perhaps the use of the page as a substitute *prima donna* is not so specious after all; at any rate Verdi forces us to believe in it.

The other principals — Samuel/Tom, Ulrica, and on the repetition, Riccardo — have their own rhythms and lines, though Riccardo's character-istic dancing dotted notes are necessarily suppressed for this passage. Here again are four separate poetic-musical sentiments, simultaneously sung over choral and orchestral support in a 'magnificent musical *tableau*' ['quadro'], as Verdi had described the ensemble in the Act Two Finale.

After a return to B*b* Major and Riccardo's stanza, a single eight-bar variant of the *ritornello* is sung, continuing the B*b* Major, with Oscar again soaring above; but because of the lower pitch it is rather less effective. That in turn makes the unexpected return to B*b* Major/b*b* minor that much the more effective: Riccardo sings the second half of his quatrain — 'Ma come fà da ridere/La lor credulità' — and on the final stress in the key word 'credulità' he goes up to a long sustained a*b'*, rather than stopping on f' as before. The principals respond in D*b* Major, and when Riccardo then drops to his usual f', they respond under it in b*b* minor. And so to the cadence preparation with Samuel/Tom's semiquavers (under chords from the other principals) suddenly sounding a lot less silly; and finally the cadence itself, in B*b* Major in the upper principal voices, while as its bass Samuel and Tom are singing a mournful g*b*-f semitone borrowed from b*b* minor.

*   *   *

Chiaroscuro: light and dark, Major and minor, ballroom and execution ground, tenor and baritone, a dance and a murder, love and death. It is the play of contrasts: in palpable ambience; in striking characters; in strong situations; but, above all, in music.

José Carreras as Gustavus at Covent Garden in 1978 (photo: Clive Barda)

1. *I copialettere di Giuseppe Verdi*, ed. A. Luzio and G. Cesari (Milan 1913), 572.

2. A manuscript copy of *Una vendetta in domino* and *Adelia degli Ademari*, in parallel columns with Verdi's annotations, was given by him to Cesare de Sanctis, and is now at the Accademia dei Lincei, Rome. Luzio's 'Il libretto del 'Ballo in maschera' massacrato dalla censura borbonica', *Carteggi verdiani* I (Rome 1935), 241-75, is a thorough account, with transcriptions of all Verdi's annotations.

3. Many of Verdi's letters to Somma were published by A. Pascolato in *Re Lear e Ballo in maschera* (Città di Castello 1913), and excerpts from Somma's letters to Verdi were published by A. Luzio in 'Le Lettere del Somma sul libretto del *Ballo in maschera*', *Carteggi verdiani* I (Rome 1935), 219-40; quotations from Somma's letters and earlier versions of his libretto text here, however, are from films of the letters themselves at the American Institute for Verdi Studies, the originals being at Villa Sant'Agata.

4. *Copialettere* op. cit., 562. The Spanish play was *Il tesoriere del rey*, by García Gutiérrez whose *El trovador* and *Simon Boccanegra* Verdi had succeeded in reducing to '*proporzioni musicabili*' earlier in the 1850s.

5. See 'Making "Macbeth" *musicabile*', in ENO Opera Guide 41 (London 1989).

6. Cammarano (1802-1852) was the librettist for Donizetti's *Lucia di Lammermoor* and many others, and for Verdi's *Il trovatore*, as well as *Luisa Miller, La battaglia di Legnano*, and *Alzira*. Rossi (1774-1855) had written for Mayr, Rossini (*Tancredi, Semiramide*), Meyerbeer, Mercadante (*Il giuramento*), and Donizetti (*Linda di Chamounix*).

7. Luzio 1935, p. 249.

8. In all treatments action 3f is a static movement, a formal set piece. At first glance this seems ludicrous: the ruler should make his escape without delay. But Scribe used the convention to stop 'real' time for purely musical purposes, and to screw up the tension: the 'musical' delay at this of all moments dramatizes the 'real' delay that allows the conspirators to stop the veiled lady and her escort.

9. Luzio 1935, 219, 220.

10. The best available example of a 'versione' made from a play is the manuscript copy in Piave's hand of Verdi's lengthy prose summary of *Simon Boccanegra*, recently re-edited by Daniela Goldin in the programme for the 1988/89 Florentine production (145-174).

11. See Julian Budden, *The operas of Verdi* I (London/New York 1973), 422, for the situation and references. The interpretation of the Act One finale of *Luisa Miller* as an aborted standard finale succession was proposed on pp. 88-89 of my "'La solita forma' and 'The uses of convention'", *Acta musicologica* 59 (1987), 65-90.

12. See John N. Black, "Salvadore Cammarano's programma for 'Il trovatore' and the problems of the finale", *Studi verdiani* II (Parma 1983), 78-107.

13. On p. 267 of Carlo Gatti's *Verdi* (Milan 1950/1951 in the 1981 reprint), we read: 'At the house of Sant'Agata, preferred by Maestro for thinking and composing, there remain the *abbozzi* [drafts] of the operas that he was creating: scanty, almost summary, for *Luisa Miller, Stiffelio, Rigoletto, Trovatore* and *Traviata*, and bit by bit more elaborate for *Vespri siciliani, Simon Boccanegra, Ballo in maschera, Don Carlos, Aida* and *Falstaff*.'
On p. 182 of Gatti's *Verdi nelle immagini* (Milan 1941) appears a photograph of the cabinet where the *abbozzi* were kept, and in 1941 Gatti also published a facsimile of the *abbozzo* for *Rigoletto*, since reprinted by the publisher Arnaldo Forni (Bologna 1978).

14. Luzio 1935, 257.

15. At the end, when the conspirators are heard offstage, the three afterbeats continue to a downbeat a few times, making a set of four, but this is purely cadential; the thematic conception and all actual thematic recurrences of the laughs are in three sets of three afterbeats.

16. See Siegmund Levarie, 'Tonal relations in Verdi's *Un ballo in maschera, 19th Century Music* II (1978/9), 143-47, esp. p. 144, col. 1. Levarie's larger claims for an overall governing organic tonality in this work seems preposterous, however; see Joseph Kerman's editorial response in the same issue, pp. 186-91; and in *19th Century Music* III (1979/80), Guy Marco's comments and Levarie's rejoinder, pp. 83-89.

Thematic Guide

Many of the themes from the opera have been identified in the articles by numbers in square brackets, which refer to the themes set out in these pages. The themes are also identified by the numbers in square brackets at the corresponding points in the libretto, so that the words can be related to the musical themes.

[1]

[2]

Allegro assai moderato

CONSPIRATORS
We pledge hat – red and pro – mise of ven – geance
E sta l'o – dio, che pre – pa – ra il fi – o,

[3]

Poco meno mosso

GUSTAVUS See – ing her there, what ec – sta – sy to
RICCARDO La ri – ve – drà nel – l'e – sta – si rag-

see her come to meet _____ me
-gian – te di pal – lo – – – re

[4] Aria: Alla vita

Andante

ANCKAR. All your des – ti – ny is smi – ling, full of
RENATO Al – la vi – ta che t'ar – ri – de di spe-

hope __ full of joy un – end – ing;
– ran – za e gau – dio pie – na,

[5] Ballata : Volta la terrea fronte

Allegretto

OSCAR

She ___ ga – zes at the stars, ___ her dark eyes gleaming :

Vol – ta la ter – re – a _____ fron-te al-le stel – le

[6] Ballata (continued)

Allegretto *f* *p* brillante

OSCAR Ah! ___ she speaks to Lu – ci – fer, they both ___ a – gree,

È con Lu – ci – fe – ro d'ac-cor – – do o – gnor!

[7]

Allegro brillante e presto

leggierissimo

GUSTAVUS Let us all go and see her to – ge – ther :

RICCARDO O – gni cu – ra si do – nia l di – let – to,

[8]

Allegro brillante e presto

GUST. So ___ then my lords and gen – tle – men, I'll

RICC. Dun – que, si – gno – ri a – – spet-to – vi, si –

be ex – pec – ting you,

gno – ri a – spet – to – vi,

[9] Invocation : Re dell'abisso

Andante sostenuto *p*

ARVIDSON Come _____ I in – voke you Lu – ci – fer,

ULRICA Re _____ dell'a – bis – so af fret – ta – ti;

42

[10]

Andante sostenuto

ARVIDSON I ___ have the po - wer,   all ___ is re-vealed to me,   no - thing is
ULRICA   nul - la, più nul - la,   più ___ nulla a-scondersi   al ___ guardo

hid - den, I _____ swear ___ all _____ is ___ re - - vealed ___ to me, I swear.
mi - o   po - - trà, ___ nul - - la ___ a - - scon - - dersi po-trà

[11]

Allegro brillante

CHRISTIAN Make way   there, I'll ask   her   to tell   me   my
SILVANO   Su, fa - te - mi lar - go,   sa-per   vo'il mio

for - tune. I serve in   the   na - vy, I'm true   to his high - ness:
fa - to. Son ser - vo   del Con - te, son suo   ma - ri - na - ro:

[12]

Allegro agitato e prestissimo

[13]

Poco più lento

p cantabile

ARVIDSON Out of   the ci - ty   in ___ the   west,
ULRICA   Del - la cit - tà al l'oc - ca - - so,

43

44

[19] Anthem: O figlio d'Inghilterra

Allegro assai sostenuto

CHORUS Hail   to   our King   and   mas - - ter,
        O   fi - glio d'In - ghil - ter - - ra,

[20] Aria: Ma dall'arido stelo

Andante

p con espress.

AMELIA From the   wil - der - ness growing a - round   me
        Ma   dal - l'a - ri - do   ste-lo di - vul - sa

[21]

Andante

p con passione

AMELIA Oh   sup - port me   and help me,   dear Lord,_____
        Deh ! mi   reg - gi, m'a - i - ta,o   Si - gnor,_____

[22]

Allegro agitato

marcate

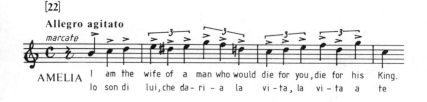

AMELIA I am the   wife of a man who would die for you, die for his   King.
        Io son di   lui, che da - ri - a la   vi - ta, la vi - ta a   te

[23] from Duet: Teco io sto (Gustavus, Amelia)

Allegretto un poco sostenuto

a mezza voce

GUSTAVUS Don't you know in my heart and my   spi-ri t_____ deep re -
RICCARDO Non sai   tu   che se l'a - ni - ma   mi - a _____ il ri -

- morse comes to pu - nish and   chide me,
- mor - so di - la - ce - ra,e   ro - de,

45

[24]

Allegro vivo

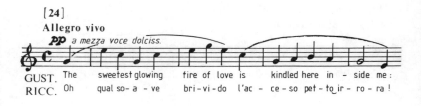

GUST. The sweetest glowing fire of love is kindled here in – side me:
RICC. Oh qual so– a – ve bri–vi–do l'ac – ce–so pet–to ir – ro – ra !

[25] from Trio : Tu qui (Amelia , Anckarstroem , Gustavus)

Presto assai

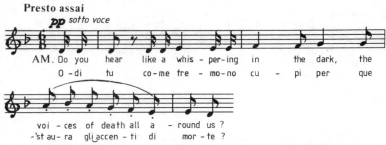

AM. Do you hear like a whis – per–ing in the dark, the
O – di tu co–me fre – mo–no cu – pi per que

voi – ces of death all a – round us ?
-'st au– ra gli accen – ti di mor – te ?

[26]

Andante mosso quasi allegretto

RIBBING Can I be dream – ing ? Strange as–sig – na – tion :
SAM Ve', se di not – te , quì col – la spo – sa

[27]

Andante mosso quasi allegretto

RIBBING A piece of gossip to spread a –round, a charming story for all the town,
& HORN E che bac–ca–no sul ca–so stra–no, e che commen–ti per la cit – tà !

[28] Aria : Morrò

Andante

AMELIA I'll die , but first I beg __ you grant me, in mer–cy, a favour:
Mor – rò , ma pri–ma in gra – zia deh! mi consenti al – me–no

[29] Aria: Eri tu

Andante sostenuto

ANCK. It was you who en –
REN. E – ri tu che mac–

_ snared and de – filed _____ my love,
– chia vi quel – là – – ni – ma,

[30]

Andante sostenuto

ANCK. Oh, the joy of my life lost for e – – ver,
REN. O dol – cez – ze per – du – te, o me – mo – – rie

[31] Vengeance Trio: (Anckarstroem, Ribbing, Horn / Renato, Sam, Tom)

Andante mosso

Let the shame we have suf – fered u – nite _____ us,
Dun – que l'on – ta di tut – ti _ sol u – – na

[32] Ballata: Di che fulgor

Allegro brillante

OSCAR On eve – ry floor the mu – sic plays and
Di che ful – gor, che mu – si – che e –

lights are bright and blaz – – ing,
– sul – te – ran le so – – – glie,

47

[33] Aria: Ma se m'è forza

Andante

GUSTAVUS Your light that shone so fair on me   is   cloud – ed now for   e – ver,
RICCARDO Ma   se   m'è for–za perderti   per sem –pre, o luce mi – a

[34]

Allegro vivissimo

[35] Canzone: Saper vorreste

Allegro

OSCAR Be – tray   his   se – cret? No,   no,   I 'll   keep it,
Sa – per   vor – re – ste di   che   si   ve – ste,

[36]

Assai moderato

con eleganza

[37]

Assai moderato

GUST. Sure_ of your love, A – me – lia,   no care can come to   grieve me:
RICC. Sin_ che tu m'ami, A – me – lia,   non cu – ro il fa – to   mi – o

Prestissimo

CHOR. Ah! Kill ___ him, the mon - ster, the monster, the mur - de-rer!
Ah, mor - te, in - fa - mia, in - fa - mia sul tra - di-tor!

[39]

Andante

grandioso

GUSTAVUS Hear me now: your King commands you : I ab - solve ___ and grant you pardon
RICCARDO Grazie a ognun signor qui so-no : tut-ti as-sol - ve il mio per -dono

Jean Watson as Arvidson, Covent Garden, 1952 (photo: Royal Opera House Archives)

49

Carol Neblett as Amelia and Carlo Bergonzi as Gustavus at San Francisco, 1985 (photo: David Powers)

A Masked Ball
Un ballo in maschera

Opera in Three Acts by Giuseppe Verdi
Text by Antonio Somma after *Gustave III* by A.E. Scribe

English translation by Edmund Tracey

The first performance of *Un ballo in maschera* was at the Teatro Apollo, Rome on February 17, 1859. The first performance in America was at the Academy of Music, New York on February 11, 1861. The first performance in Britain was at the Lyceum, London, on June 15, 1861.

This performing translation was made for a new production by English National Opera at the London Coliseum on September 14, 1989, for which the Swedish location and names (following the original intentions of the composer and librettist) were chosen. As a result the English diverges from the Italian libretto as to the names of the characters, and in details of title and place.

The layout and scene divisions follow the libretto established by Luigi Baldacci in *Tutti i libretti di Verdi*, (Garzanti, 1975). There are, however, numerous discrepancies between that libretto and the words Verdi finally set to music; so the Italian words printed here are those in the first edition of the score. The stage directions are also from the score, and are literal translations which are not part of the ENO translation or production. The musical sections (which are not numbered in the printed score) are ranged left. The numbers in square brackets refer to the Thematic Guide.

CHARACTERS

Riccardo *Earl of Warwick governor of Boston* [*Conte di Warwick*]	Gustavus III *King of Sweden*	*tenor*
Renato *a Creole, his secretary, Amelia's husband*	Count Anckarstroem *his secretary*	*baritone*
Amelia	Amelia	*soprano*
Ulrica *a fortune teller, of a black race*	Mademoiselle Arvidson	*mezzo-soprano*
Oscar *a page*	Oscar	*soprano*
Silvano *a sailor*	Christian	*bass/baritone*
Samuel } *enemies of the Earl* Tom	Count Ribbing Count Horn	*bass* *bass*
A judge	A judge	*tenor*
A servant to Amelia	A servant to Amelia	*tenor*

Deputies, Officers, Sailors, Guards, Men, Women and Children of the Populace, Gentlemen, Followers of Samuel and Tom [Ribbing and Horn], Servants, Maskers, and Dancing Couples.

The action takes place in and around Boston, Massachussetts towards the end of the seventeenth century.

In this English translation, as explained on the previous page, the characters' names are those for the Swedish setting which takes place at the court of Gustavus III, King of Sweden, at the end of the eighteenth century.

Prelude [1, 2, 3]

Act One

Scene One. *A room in the King's palace. At the back, the doors into his rooms. It is morning. Deputies, Gentlemen, Members of the Populace, Officers, Counts Ribbing and Horn and their followers are waiting for the King.*

Introduction.

OFFICERS AND GENTLEMEN

Heaven guard you and sweet sleep restore you,	[1]	Posa in pace, a' bei sogni ristora,
o Gustavus, our noble young lord.		O Riccardo, il tuo nobile cor.
As your shield we all promise to guard you,		A te scudo su questa dimora
to your service we pledge you our word.		Sta d'un vergine mondo l'amor.

RIBBING, HORN AND THEIR FOLLOWERS

We pledge hatred and promise of vengeance,	[2]	E sta l'odio, che prepara il fio,
for the men you have condemned to die.		Ripensando ai caduti per te.
You are hoping that we will forget them,		Come speri, disceso l'obblio
men who died and are now in their graves.		Sulle tombe infelice non è.

Scene Two. *Oscar in the King's apartments, then Gustavus.*

Scene and Entrance [*aria di sortita*].

OSCAR

Our King Gustavus!   S'avanza il Conte.

Enter Gustavus, greeting those present.

GUSTAVUS

My friends I greet you . . . my soldiers.   Amici miei . . . soldati.
receiving various petitions from the deputies
It gives me joy to see you here. I'll take   E voi del par diletti a me! Porgete;
them:
it's what I was expecting. I know I   A me s'aspetta; io deggio
must take care of my sons, and your   Su' miei figli vegliar, perchè sia pago
petitions
I'll consider, I promise.   Ogni voto, se giusto.
Kings have to find a way to love their   Bello il poter non è, che de' soggetti
subjects
and comfort them in sorrow . . . seek to   Le lagrime non terge, e ad incorrotta
find untainted
glory and honour.   Gloria non mira.

OSCAR
to Gustavus
        Would you like to read   Leggere vi piaccia
The list of names for your party?   Delle danze l'invito.

GUSTAVUS
        You've not forgotten   Avresti alcuna
a single fair young beauty?   Beltà dimenticato?

OSCAR
handing him a paper
        All are invited.   Eccovi i nomi.

GUSTAVUS
reading, aside

Amelia! Her name is there ... Dearest
name! Ah, it is she
who so enchants me I forget I am a King.

Amelia ... ah, dessa ancor! l'anima mia

In lei rapita ogni grandezza oblia!

Seeing her there, what ecstasy,
to see her come to meet me,
and then to hear her greet me
in tender words of love.
O starry night, come sweetly down
and blaze in all your glory:
she is the star before me,
the only star before me.

[3] La rivedrà nell'estasi
Raggiante di pallore ...
E qui sonar d'amore
La sua parola udrà.
O dolce notte, scendere
Tu puoi gemmata a festa;
Ma la mia stella è questa;
Questa, che il ciel non ha!

OSCAR, OFFICERS AND GENTLEMEN

With generous affection
he thinks about his people,
he's lost in deep reflection,
his heart and soul are true.

Con generoso affetto
Entro se stesso assorto,
Il nostro bene oggetto
De' suoi pensier farà.

RIBBING, HORN AND THEIR FOLLOWERS
softly

We'll bide our time, today we
must leave our prey behind us;
but very soon he'll find us
agreed on what to do.

L'ora non è, chè tutto
Qui d'operar ne toglie.
Dalle nemiche soglie
Meglio l'uscir sarà.

Scene and Cantabile.

GUSTAVUS
to Oscar

Go with the others outside ... I will
call you.

Il cenno mia di là con essi attendi.

They all leave. Oscar, the last to go, encounters Anckarstroem on the threshold.

OSCAR
to Anckarstroem

The way is always open to you.

Libero è il varco a voi.

He leaves.

Scene Three. *Gustavus and Anckarstroem.*

ANCKARSTROEM
aside

Why does he look so sad?

Deh, come triste appar!

GUSTAVUS
aside

Amelia!

Amelia!

ANCKARSTROEM

Highness ...

Conte ...

GUSTAVUS
aside

Ah God, can he have heard me?

Oh ciel! lo sposo suo!

ANCKARSTROEM

You seem upset,
my lord, yet throughout your kingdom
the people cheer your name and glory.

Turbato il mio
Signor, mentre dovunque il nome suo
Inclito suona?

54

That says much for my glory,
nothing for my heart. A secret, bitter worry
torments me.

Per la gloria è molto,
Nulla pel cor. Segreta, acerba cura
M'opprime.

ANCKARSTROEM

Please trust me.

E d'onde?

GUSTAVUS

I do, but still . . .

Ah no . . . non più . . .

ANCKARSTROEM

I know the
cause of your fear.

Dirolla
Io la cagion.

GUSTAVUS
aside

You know it?

Gran Dio!

ANCKARSTROEM

Believe me . . .

So tutto . . .

GUSTAVUS

Go on.

E che?

ANCKARSTROEM

Believe me.
Inside this very chamber
your safety is in danger.

So tutto.
Già questa soglia istessa
Non t'è securo asilo.

GUSTAVUS

Continue.

Prosegui.

ANCKARSTROEM

A vile group of traitors
are plotting in the shadows:
they really mean to kill you.

Un reo disegno
Nell'ombre si matura,
I giorni tuoi minaccia.

GUSTAVUS
joyfully

Is this why you are worried?
Come, tell me more . . .

Ah! gli è di ciò che parli?
Altro non sai?

ANCKARSTROEM

I have the list of names here.

Se udir ti piace i nomi.

GUSTAVUS

No matter. I just despise them.

Che importa? Io li disprezzo.

ANCKARSTROEM

I must reveal the truth.

Svelarli è mio dover.

GUSTAVUS

Never: condemn my
own courtiers, put them all to death? I
will not.
Enough! My people love me,
they will protect me: I pray to God to
save me.

Taci: nel sangue
Contaminarmi allor dovrei. Non fia,
Nol vo'. Del popol mio
L'amor mi guardi e mi protegga Iddio.

ANCKARSTROEM

All your destiny is smiling,
full of hope, full of joy unending;
many thousands of your people
on your safety are depending.
If we lose you when we need you,
then our country's hope will die.

[4] Alla vita che t'arride
Di speranze e gaudio piena,
D'altre mille e mille vite
Il destino s'incatena!
Te perduto, ov'è la patria
Col suo splendido avvenir?

Do you think there is no danger,
do you feel no sword can strike you,
just because we shield and guard you
and because your people love you?
We may love, but those who hate you
strike their blows and honour defy.

E sarà dovunque, sempre
Chiuso il varco alle ferite,
Perchè scudo del tuo petto
È del popolo l'affetto?
Dell'amor più desto è l'odio
Le sue vittime a colpir.

Scene Four. *Oscar, then a Judge and others.*

OSCAR
at the doorway

The judge is waiting.　　　　　　　　　　Il primo Giudice.

GUSTAVUS

　　　Admit him.　　　　　　　　　　　S'avanzi.

Scene and Ballata.

JUDGE
handing him dispatches to sign
　　　Your Highness!　　　　　　　　　　　　　　　Conte!

GUSTAVUS

An order — to banish some poor
　woman. Who is she?
Where does she come from? Is she
　guilty?

Che leggo! Il bando ad una donna. Or
　d'onde?
Qual è il suo nome? Di che rea?

JUDGE

　　　Her name is　　　　　　　　　　　　　　　S'appella
Arvidson. She's a crazy,
dangerous gypsy.

Ulrica dell'immondo
Sangue de' negri.*

OSCAR

The people come from far and near,
throngng to see her. She is brilliant at
　telling
you your fortune.

Intorno a cui s'affollano
Tutte le stirpi. Del futuro l'alta

Divinatrice . . .

JUDGE

　　　She attracts all the vilest　　　　　　　　Che nell'antro abbietto
scum in the city; I am sure she is
　plotting
with traitors too. I ask that she be
　banished:
I know that she is guilty.

Chiama i peggiori, d'ogni reo consiglio

Sospetta già. Dovuto è a lei l'esiglio,

Nè muta il voto mio.

GUSTAVUS
to Oscar

You don't agree?　　　　　　　　　Che ne di' tu?

OSCAR

　　　I'd like to be her champion.　　　　　　Difenderla vogl'io.

She gazes at the stars,
her dark eyes gleaming:
Venus as well as Mars,
she knows their meaning.
Here comes a young maid,
her future seeking:
'What do the stars say
about my love?
Is it sad or happy,
Oh, what can you see?'

[5]　Volta la terrea,
Fronte alle stelle,
Come sfavilla
La sua pupilla,
Quando alle belle
Il fin predice
Mesto o felice
Dei loro amor!
Mesto o felice
Dei loro amor!

* Lit. of filthy Negro blood.

56

She speaks to Lucifer, they both agree!	[6] È con Lucifero D'accordo ognor!

GUSTAVUS

And does old Lucifer charge her a fee?	Che vaga coppia, Che protettor!

OSCAR

She knows what is to be for she can read it, she gives you warning so you can heed it. Sail on the dark sea by night or morning; fight for your country to keep it free. The ending, the ending, she will foresee. She speaks to Lucifer, they both agree!	[5] Chi la profetica Sua gonna afferra, O passi 'l mare, Voli alla guerra, Le sue vicende Soavi, amare Da questa apprende Nel dubbio cor. Da questa apprende Nel dubbio cor. [6] È con Lucifero D'accordo ognor!

Stretta of the Introduction.

JUDGE

She must be banished.	Sia condannata.

OSCAR
turning to the King

I plead for her acquittal.	Assolverla degnate.

GUSTAVUS

Well then, summon the others: they'll hear what I decide.	Ebben: tutti chiamate: Or v'apro un mio pensier.

Oscar and Anckarstroem go to invite the others to re-enter.

Scene Five. *Counts Ribbing and Horn and their followers, Gentlemen and Officers.*

GUSTAVUS

My friends, I now invite you to visit Madame Arvidson, but wearing other clothing; I shall go too.	Signori, oggi d'Ulrica Alla magion v'invito, Ma sotto altro vestito; Io là sarò.

ANCKARSTROEM

Go there? You're sure?	Davver? Davver?

GUSTAVUS

I know it will amuse me.	Si, vo' gusta la scena.

ANCKARSTROEM

I fear a certain danger.	L'idea non è prudente.

OSCAR

The plan is really splendid and sure to make us laugh.	La trovo anzi eccellente, Feconda di piacer.

ANCKARSTROEM

Supposing there is someone there who knows you?	Te ravvisar taluno Ivi potria.

GUSTAVUS

What nonsense!	Qual tema!

RIBBING AND HORN
sneering

He's scared of his own shadow, this pillar of the state!	Ve', ve', di tutto trema Codesto consiglier.

GUSTAVUS
to Oscar

You'll have to find some clothes for me, as a fisherman.	E tu m'appronta un abito Da pescator.

RIBBING, HORN AND THEIR FOLLOWERS

This may be just the stroke of luck we need to carry out our plan!	Chi sa ... Che alla vendetta l'adito Non s'apra alfin colà?

GUSTAVUS

Let us all go and see her together; an adventure of laughter and pleasure. We will mix with the people around us as we laugh all our worries away.	[7] Ogni cura si doni al dileto E s'accorra nel magico tetto: Tra la folla de' creduli ognuno S'abbandoni e folleggi con me.

ANCKARSTROEM

If we go it would surely be better to beware of the dangers around us; we must care for our lord and protector so that nothing may harm him today.	E s'accorra, ma vegli il sospetto Sui perigli che fremono intorno, Ma protegga il magnanimo petto A chi nulla paventa per sè.

OSCAR

She has so many magical stories; I will ask her to tell me my fortune: and I know when I tell her my worries, she is sure to have something to say.	L'indovina ne dice di belle, E sta ben che l'interroghi anch'io; Sentirò se m'arridon le stelle, Di che sorte benefica m'è.

GUSTAVUS

So then, my lords and gentlemen, I'll be expecting you, incognito, yes, at three. We'll go to hear the oracle, we'll worship at the shrine, we all will bow the knee.	[8] Dunque signori, aspettovi, Signori aspettovi, Incognito, alle tre Nell'antro dell'oracolo, Della gran maga al piè, Della gran maga al piè.

RIBBING, HORN AND THEIR FOLLOWERS

Let us never forget our intention, never lose any chances of action; and it may be today we will strike him, with a blow that will set us all free.	Senza posa vegliamo all' intento, Né si perda ove scocchi 'l momento; Forse l'astro che regge il suo fato Nell'abisso là spegnersi de'.

ALL

We will be there to wait on you, incognito, yes, at three, we'll go to hear the oracle, we all will bow the knee.	Teco sarem di subito, Incogniti alle tre, Nell'antro dell'oracolo, Della gran maga al piè.

Scene Six. *The dwelling of the fortune-teller. To the left is a hearth; the fire is alight, and the magic cauldron smokes on a tripod; on the same side is an opening to a dark recess. On the right is a staircase which turns and disappears out of sight; at its foot, downstage, is a secret door. At the back is the entrance by the main door, with wide windows at the side. In the middle is a rough table, and hanging from the roof and the walls are the objects and instruments appropriate for such a place.*

Invocation.

WOMEN AND CHILDREN

Quiet, she's talking to spirits around her, she will soon hear the demon speaking inside her.	Zitti, l'incanto non dèssi turbare. Il dimonio tra breve halle a parlare.

ARVIDSON
as if possessed

Come, I invoke you, Lucifer, fly here, your secrets telling.	[9] Re dell'abisso, affrettati, Precipita per l'etra,

58

Do not release your thunder	Senza librar la folgore
until you enter my dwelling.	Il tetto mio penètra.
Three times has the owl been hooting	Omai tre volte l'upupa
his warning long and low;	Dall'alto sospirò;
bright salamander's hissing flames	La salamandra ignivora
have told their tale of woe . . .	Tre volte sibillò . . .
Three times a wailing from the tomb	E delle tombe il gemito
has sounded deep and slow.	Tre volte a me parlò.

Scene Seven. *Gustavus enters, dressed as a fisherman. He makes his way through the crowd, unrecognised by anyone.*

Scene.

GUSTAVUS

I'm here before them!	Arrivo il primo!

WOMEN AND CHILDREN
pushing him away

Be off and leave us!	Villano, dà indietro.

He moves away, laughing. The stage darkens a little.

GUSTAVUS

Oh, what a strange glow to lighten the darkness!	Oh, come qui tutto riluce di tetro!

ARVIDSON
declaiming ecstatically

The god! The god! I feel him now,	È lui! è lui! ne' palpiti
feel all his power returning:	Come risento adesso
his mighty arms are holding me,	La voluttà riardere
in dark embrace fiercely burning!	Del suo tremendo amplesso!
The torch of fate is glowing,	La face del futuro
his left hand holds it high,	Nella sinistra egli ha.
he grants me my wish to know him,	M'arrise al mio scongiuro,
to conjure his reply:	Rifolgorar la fa:
I have the power, all is revealed to me, [10]	Nulla, più nulla ascondersi
nothing is hidden, I swear!	Al guardo mio potrà.

She beats the ground and disappears.

ALL

Oh, what a magician!	Evviva la maga!

ARVIDSON
from below

Be silent!	Silenzio!

Scene Eight. *Christian breaks through the crowd.*

CHRISTIAN

Make way there, I'll ask her to tell me my fortune. [11]	Su, fatemi largo, saper vo' il mio fato.
I serve in the navy, I'm true to His Highness:	Son servo del Conte: son suo marinaro:
I've fought in his battles, I've been near to drowning,	La morte per esso più volte ho sfidato;
I've served him for ten years with no word of kindness,	Tre lustri son corsi del vivere amaro,
I've served him for ten years with nothing to show.	Tre lustri che nulla s'è fato per me.

ARVIDSON
reappearing

So ask me . . .	E chiedi?

CHRISTIAN

I want you to tell me what future
awaits me.

Qual sorte pel sangue versato
M'attende.

GUSTAVUS
aside

He speaks like a man who is loyal.

Favella da franco soldato.

ARVIDSON
to Christian

I'll tell you.

La mano.

CHRISTIAN
giving her his hand

You'll read it?

Prendete.

ARVIDSON
looking at his hand

I've good news to tell:
you'll soon get promotion and money
as well.

Rallegrati omai:
In breve dell'oro e un grado t'avrai.

Gustavus takes out a roll of paper and writes on it.

CHRISTIAN

You mean it?

Scherzate?

ARVIDSON

I promise.

Va' pago.

GUSTAVUS
putting the paper in Christian's pocket while he does not notice

She must tell the truth.

Mentire non de'.

CHRISTIAN

A joyful prediction deserves a reward.

A fausto presagio ben vuolsi mercé.

searching, he discovers the paper, which he reads ecstatically

'Gustavus, to his dear friend and
captain Christian.'
I'm dreaming, a wallet with money, a
commission!

'Riccardo al suo caro Silvano Uffiziale.'

Per bacco! Non sogno! Dell'oro ed un
grado!

WOMEN AND CHILDREN

A marvel, a marvel, oh, what a magician,
she scatters good fortune and joy to
us all!

Evviva la nostra Sibilla immortale,
Che spande su tutti ricchezze e piacer!

CHRISTIAN, WOMEN AND CHILDREN

Who's knocking?

Si batte!

A knock at the little door is heard; Arvidson opens it and a servant enters.

GUSTAVUS
aside

Who is it? I see from his livery
a servant of Amelia.

Che vego! Sull'uscio segreto
Un servo d'Amelia.

SERVANT
softly to Arvidson, but in Gustavus's hearing

Listen: my mistress
desires your assistance in private, she
asks you
to see her and give her your help and
advice.

Sentite: la mia
Signora, che aspetta là fuori, vorria

Pregarvi in segreto d'arcano parer.

GUSTAVUS

Amelia!

Amelia!

Admit her; I'll tell them to leave me.   S'inoltri, ch'io tutti allontano.

GUSTAVUS

Not I!   Non me.

He hides in the recess. She turns to the onlookers.

ARVIDSON

If you want me to answer you all,   Perchè possa rispondere a voi
I must speak to Satan and ask his   E d'uopo che innanzi m'abbocchi a
  assistance.   Satana.
Now leave me, all leave me, I must find   Uscite: lasciate ch'io scruti nel ver.
  the truth.

WOMEN AND CHILDREN

We'll leave her, all leave her, she must   Usciamo: si lasci che scruti nel ver.
  find the truth.

While all leave, Gustavus stays behind.

Scene Nine. *Amelia, Arvidson and Gustavus in the background.*

Scene and Terzetto. [12]

ARVIDSON

What causes your distress?   Che v'agita così?

AMELIA

A secret, bitter   Segreta, acerba
Torture aroused by love . . .   Cura che amor destò . . .

GUSTAVUS
from his hiding place

Amelia!   Che ascolto!

ARVIDSON

And what   E voi
can I do?   Cercate?

AMELIA

Help me! Take away for ever   Pace . . . svellermi dal petto
this fatal longing, this desire that rules   Chi sì fatale e desiato impera!
  my heart.
One who is higher than all — chosen   Lui, che su tutti il ciel arbitro pose.
  by God Himself.

GUSTAVUS
to himself, with a lively expression of joy

Dearest beloved!   Anima mia!

ARVIDSON

You can forget him. I know a   L'oblio v'è dato. Arcane
herb whose juices have a magical power;   Stille conosco d'una magic' erba,
it could control your heart. Just one   Che rinnovella il cor. Ma chi n'ha
  condition: d'uopo
you have to pick the herb yourself,   Spiccarla debbe di sua man nel fitto
  upon the
stroke of midnight . . . in a place   Delle notti . . . Funereo
full of horror.   È il loco.

AMELIA

Where is it?   Ov'è?

ARVIDSON

You'd dare to   L'osate
go there?   Voi?

AMELIA
resolutely

Yes, I have to do it.

Sì, qual esso sia.

ARVIDSON

Hear what I tell you.

Dunque ascoltate.

Out of the city, in the west,
beyond the dark horizon,
there where the moonlight shines above
the field of execution . . .
The herb that can restore you
grows in a place of horror:
there where the guilty pay the price
and draw their long last breath!

[13] Della città all'occaso,
Là dove al tetro lato
Batte la luna pallida
Sul campo abbominato . . .
Abbarbica gli stami
A quelle pietre infami,
Ove la colpa scontasi
Coll'ultimo sospir!

AMELIA

My God, how fearful!

Mio Dio! qual loco!

ARVIDSON

You look so pale . . .
I see your hands are trembling.

Attonita
E già tremante siete?

GUSTAVUS

How can I help?

Povero cor!

ARVIDSON

You're cold as ice . . .

V'esanima?

AMELIA

With terror . . .

Agghiaccio . . .

ARVIDSON

So will you dare it?

E l'oserete?

AMELIA

I know my solemn duty . . .
Somehow I'll find the courage.

Se tale è il dover mio
Troverò possa anch'io.

ARVIDSON

At midnight?

Stanotte?

AMELIA

Yes.

Sì.

GUSTAVUS
aside

I'll follow,
You shall not go alone.

Non sola,
Ché te degg'io seguir.

AMELIA

I beg of you, dear Lord God,
to grant the grace to cleanse me,
and drive away for evermore
this guilty love in my heart.

[14] Consentimi, o Signore,
Virtù ch'io lavi 'l core,
E l'infiammato palpito
Nel petto mio sopir.

ARVIDSON

Go, never fear, the magic
herb will end all your weeping.
Go now and taste oblivion,
and soothe your grieving heart.

Va', non tremar, l'incanto
Inaridisce il pianto.
Osa e berrai nel farmaco
L'oblio de' tuoi martir.

GUSTAVUS

Burning with love I'll follow,
yes, into Hell's dark hollow.
I only breathe, Amelia,
sighs from your grieving heart.

Ardo, e seguirla ho fisso
Se fosse nell'abisso,
Pur ch'io respiri, Amelia,
L'aura de' tuoi sospir.

VOICES
offstage

Daughter of Satan, where are you hidden?

Figlia d'averno, schiudi la chiostra,

knocking at the door

No more delaying, come when you're bidden.

E tarda meno a noi ti mostra.

ARVIDSON
to Amelia

Better go this way.

Presto, partite.

AMELIA

At midnight.

Stanotte.

ARVIDSON

At midnight, remember, quickly and leave me!

Addio . . .
Partite, presto partite!

AMELIA

I'll leave you!

Addio!

GUSTAVUS

I'll follow: you shall not go alone!

Non sola:
Ché te degg'io seguir.

Amelia escapes by the secret door.

Scene Ten. *Arvidson opens the main door; Ribbing, Horn (and their followers), Oscar, Gentlemen and Officers, in strange disguises, enter; Gustavus joins them.*

Scene and Canzone.

RIBBING, HORN AND GENTLEMEN

Daughter of Satan, weave us a spell.
Tell us the future.

Su, profetessa, monta il treppiè.
Canta il futuro.

OSCAR

Where is the King?

Ma il Conte ov'è?

GUSTAVUS
to Oscar

Silence, I order you. Keep it a secret.

Taci, nascondile che qui son io.

to Arvidson

Sibyl of Hades, tell me my future,
what do the stars say, tell me the truth.

Or tu, Sibilla, che tutto sai,
Della mia stella mi parlerai.

RIBBING, HORN AND GENTLEMEN

Tell him his future!

Canta il futuro!

GUSTAVUS

Oh, say if the ocean
safely will guard me,
and why with such tears
does my lady regard me.
With kisses she pays me,
and then she betrays me.
My sails are in tatters,
my mind in confusion
and yet I will conquer
the storm and the ocean.
I'll dare in their fury
both heaven and hell.
Reveal what will happen,
and let it be frightening!
No tempest subdues me,

[15] Di' tu se fedele
Il flutto m'aspetta,
Se molle di pianto
La donna diletta
Dicendomi addio
Tradì l'amor mio.
Con lacere vele
E l'alma in tempesta,
I solchi so franger
Dell'onda funesta,
L'averno ed il cielo
Irati sfidar.
Sollecita esplora,
Divina gli eventi:
Non possono i fulmin,

no thunder or lightning;
my love for the sea
even death cannot quell!

La rabbia de' venti,
La morte, l'amore
Sviarmi dal mar.

ALL THE OTHERS

No tempest subdues me,
no thunder or lightning;
not death and not love
my passion can quell.

Non possono i fulmin,
La rabbia de' venti,
La morte, l'amore
Svialo dal mar.

GUSTAVUS

I sail on the ocean
that nurses and rocks me,
I'm blown by a tempest
that whistles and shocks me.
I sing in its wild mood,
the songs of my childhood,
the music we sang as
our journey was starting.
The tears and the sighs
and the kisses at parting
inspiring new vigour
and hope in my heart.
Reveal what will happen
and tell us your story.
We're ready to welcome
our death and our glory,
for nowhere inside us
can fear play a part!

Sull'agile prora
Che m'agita in grembo,
Se scosso mi sveglio
Ai fischi del nembo,
Ripeto fra tuoni
Le dolci canzoni,
Le dolci canzoni,
Del tetto natìo,
Che i baci ricordan
Dell' ultimo addio,
E tutte riaccendon
Le forze del cor.
Su, dunque, risuoni
La tua profezia;
Di' ciò che può sorger
Dal fato qual sia;
Nell'anime nostre
Non entra terror.

ALL THE OTHERS

For nowhere inside us
can fear play a part!

Nell'anime nostre
Non entra terror.

ARVIDSON

Those are bold words to hear from a stranger,
but be careful or you may regret them:
if the powers of darkness resent them,
bitter tears will not wash them away.
If you scorn and defy what is written,
there is always the devil to pay.

Chi voi siate, l'audace parola

Può nel pianto prorompere un giorno,
Se chi sforza l'arcano soggiorno
Va la colpa nel duolo a lavar,
Se chi sfida il suo fato insolente,
Deve l'onta nel fato scontar.

GUSTAVUS

Then we'll pay him!

Orsù, amici.

RIBBING

And who is to lead us?

Ma il primo chi fia?

OSCAR

I will!

Io!

He gives his hand to Arvidson.

GUSTAVUS
giving his hand

Let me have the honour.

L'onore a me cedi.

OSCAR

You may have it!

E lo sia.

ARVIDSON
solemnly, examining his hand

Here's a strong hand and noble, and here I

È la destra d'un grande, vissuto

see that Mars is his planet.	Sotto l'astro di Marte.

OSCAR

| She's right on | Nel vero |
| the target. | Ella colse. |

GUSTAVUS

| Be quiet. | Tacete. |

ARVIDSON
drawing back from him

| Ah, how fearful! | Infelice ... |
| Go, I cannot ... don't ask me I beg! | Va, mi lascia ... non chieder di più. |

GUSTAVUS

| Yes, continue. | Su, prosegui. |

ARVIDSON

| No, pity me! | No ... lasciami. |

GUSTAVUS

| Tell me! | Parla! |

ARVIDSON
evading him

| Please, I beg you. | Te ne prego. |

RIBBING, HORN, OSCAR AND GENTLEMEN
to Arvidson

| You must tell him the rest! | Eh, finiscila omai! |

GUSTAVUS

| I command you. | Te lo impongo. |

ARVIDSON

| Well then, soon you will die. | Ebben, presto morrai. |

GUSTAVUS

| If I die in the field, I am happy. | Se sul campo d'onor, ti so grado. |

ARVIDSON
with more force

| No, a friend's hand will strike you ... | No ... per man d'un amico ... |

OSCAR

| Great Heaven! | Gran Dio! |
| Fatal word! | Quale orror! |

RIBBING, HORN, OSCAR AND GENTLEMEN

| Fatal word! | Quale orror! |

ARVIDSON

| Fate has written it so. | Così scritto à lassù. |

GUSTAVUS
looking around him

She may be mad or does she joke,	[16] È scherzo od è follia
prophetic words she spoke.	Siffatta profezia:
But how it makes me laugh at them,	Ma come fa da ridere
the way they take her part!	La lor credulità!

ARVIDSON
walking in front of Ribbing and Horn

Ah, you good sirs, you hear me,	Ah voi, signori, a queste
believe my fatal prophecy.	Parole mie funeste
You do not dare to laugh at me,	Voi non osate ridere;
what have you in your heart?	Che dunque in cor vi sta?

RIBBING AND HORN

staring at Arvidson

Her words are arrows and lances,	[17] La sua parola è dardo,
there's lightning in her glances;	È fulmine lo sguardo;
her lord and master Lucifer	Dal confidente dèmone
will tell her what to say.	Tutto costei risà.

OSCAR AND GENTLEMEN

Is this how fate is ordered,	[18] E tal fia dunque il fato
that he must now be murdered?	Ch'ei cada assassinato?
I cannot bear to think of it;	Al sol pensarci l'anima
I shudder in my heart.	Abbrividendo va.

Scene and Anthem — First Finale.

GUSTAVUS

So, finish off the story.	Finisci il vaticinio.
Who is the man to strike the blow?	Di', chi fia dunque l'uccisor?

ARVIDSON

The man who	Chi primo
is first to take you by the hand.	Tua man quest'oggi stringerà.

GUSTAVUS

with vivacity

A splendid thought!	Benissimo!

He offers his hand to those standing around him but no one dares touch it.

So which of you is ready	Qual è di voi, che provi
to prove that she is lying?	L'oracolo bugiardo?
You're frightened!	Nessuno!

Scene Eleven. *Anckarstroem appears at the entrance. Gustavus runs to him, and shakes him by the hand.*

GUSTAVUS

Welcome, sir.	Eccolo.

OSCAR, RIBBING, HORN AND GENTLEMEN

It can't be!	È desso!

RIBBING AND HORN

to their followers

How lucky: now we can breathe again.	Respiro: il caso ne salvò.

OSCAR AND GENTLEMEN

to Arvidson

The oracle	L'oracolo
was lying.	mentiva.

GUSTAVUS

Yes: you see the man who greeted me	Sì: perchè la man che stringo
is my most faithful friend and comrade.	E del più fido amico mio.

ANCKARSTROEM

Gustavus!	Riccardo!

ARVIDSON

recognising the King

Your Highness!	Il Conte!

GUSTAVUS

to Arvidson

All your powers could not instruct you	Nè, chi fossi, il genio tuo
who or what I am, or how the lawyers urged me	Ti rivelò, nè che voleano al bando
to sentence you to exile.	Oggi dannarti.

66

Exile?   Me?

GUSTAVUS
throwing her a purse
Don't worry, here's money.   T'acqueta e prendi.

ARVIDSON
How generous you are; yet there are   Magnanimo tu se', ma v'ha fra loro
traitors
in this crowd. Yes, there is danger . . .   Il traditor! più d'uno forse . . .

RIBBING AND HORN
Great Heaven!   Gran Dio!

GUSTAVUS
No more.   Non più.

PEOPLE
in the distance, offstage
Long live Gustavus!   Viva Riccardo!

ALL
They hail him!   Quai voci?

Scene Twelve. *Christian to those with him, from the back, on the threshold.*

CHRISTIAN
The King, make haste to greet him; the   È lui, ratti movete, è lui:
King:
we greet you, our noble friend and father.   Il nostro amico e padre.
Sailors, men and women of the populace crowd together at the doorway.
Come in with me and kneel in loyal   Tutti con me chinatevi al suo piede
homage:
sing him our praises, pledge our faith   E l'inno suoni della nostra fè.
today.

PEOPLE
Hail to our King and master,   [19] O figlio d'Inghilterra,*
hail to our noble father!   Amor di questa terra!
Health and good fortune smile on you,   Reggi felice, arridano
may you rejoice in glory today.   Gloria e salute a te.

OSCAR
A joy beyond all measure,   Il più superbo alloro,
fairer than any treasure,   Che vince ogni tesoro,
will sound and then re-echo   Alla tua chioma intreccian
your people's love today.   Riconoscenza e fè.

GUSTAVUS
Away with dark suspicion,   E posso alcun sospetto
away with a traitor's mission;   Alimentar nel petto,
a thousand hearts on fire to go   Se mille cuori battono
and die for me today.   Per immolarsi a me?

ARVIDSON
He would not heed my warning,   Non crede al proprio fato,
his fate is to die in torment.   Ma pur morrà piagato;
He ridiculed my warning,   Sorrise al mio presagio,
but he has one foot in the grave.   Ma nella fossa ha il piè.

ANCKARSTROEM
Here in the cries of gladness,   Ma la sventura è cosa
death may be in the shadows: Pur ne' trionfi ascosa,

---

* Lit. O son of England!

somewhere a smiling hypocrite
sharpens his knife today.

Là dove il fato ipocrita
Veli una rea mercè.

RIBBING, HORN AND THEIR FOLLOWERS
among themselves

Kill him and end this babble;
see how the servile rabble
stupidly bow and fawn on him,
fawn on their god today.

Chiude al ferir la via
Questa servil genia,
Che sta lambendo l'idolo,
E che non sa il perchè.

The curtain falls.

Placido Domingo as Gustavus at Covent Garden, 1975 (Royal Opera House Archives)

68

Act Two

Prelude, Scene and Aria.

Amelia appears at the top of the hill. During the Prelude, she kneels and prays. Then she rises, and gradually comes down the hill.

AMELIA

In this horrible field of retribution,	Ecco l'orrido campo ove s'accoppia
death and evil are coupled.	Al delitto la morte!
Over there are the gallows ...	Ecco là le colonne ...
The magic herb is growing there. Go forward!	La pianta è là, verdeggia al piè. S'innoltri.
Ah, how my heart is frozen!	Ah, mi si aggela il core!
Even the steps I take myself, everything fills me with fearful dread and aching terror!	Sino il rumor de' passi miei, qui tutto M'empie di raccapriccio e di terrore!
And what if I should perish?	E se perir dovessi?
I perish! Well then, let me achieve my duty,	Perire! ebben! quando la sorte mia,
and let me meet my fate. God help me: so be it.	Il mio dover tal è, s'adempia, e sia!

She begins to move again.

From the wilderness growing around me [20]	Ma dall'arido stelo divulsa
I will gather the flower that brings peace.	Come avrò di mia mano quell'erba,
Though my dark secret terrors confound me,	E che dentro la mente convulsa
this sweet remedy will root out my love.	Quell'eterea sembianza morrà,
What is left you for life to restore,	Che ti resta, perduto l'amor ...
what is left you when you love no more?	Che ti resta, mio povero cor!
Oh, what weeping, what force pulls me backward?	Oh! chi piange, qual forza m'arretra?
What forbids me this cheerless dark pathway?	M'attraversa la squallida via?
Come, have courage, let me turn into stone;	Su coraggio ... e tu fatti di pietra,
heart, be faithful, your weeping must cease,	Non tradirmi, dal pianto ristà;
or stop beating, my heart, evermore.	O finisci di battere e muor,
Break forever, when you love no more!	T'annienta, mio povero cor!

Midnight strikes.

It is midnight! Ah, a phantom ... it is rising,	Mezzanotte! Ah, che veggio? Una testa
I can see it, I hear it, it is sighing!	Di sotterra si leva ... e sospira!
Ah, from its wild eyes there are flashes of anger,	Ha negli occhi il baleno dell'ira
how it stares with a terrible fire!	E m'affisa e terribile sta!

She falls to her knees.

Oh, support me and help me, dear Lord, [21]	Deh! mi reggi, m'aita, o Signor,
and have pity on me evermore!	Miserere d'un povero cor!

Scene Two. *Gustavus and Amelia. Gustavus unexpectedly appears.*

Duet.

<table>
<tr><td colspan="2" align="center">GUSTAVUS</td></tr>
<tr><td>Take my hand!</td><td>Teco io sto.</td></tr>
</table>

<table>
<tr><td colspan="2" align="center">AMELIA</td></tr>
<tr><td align="center">Great Heaven!</td><td align="center">Gran Dio!</td></tr>
</table>

<table>
<tr><td colspan="2" align="center">GUSTAVUS</td></tr>
<tr><td align="right">Amelia,</td><td align="right">Ti calma!</td></tr>
<tr><td>you are trembling.</td><td>Di che temi?</td></tr>
</table>

<table>
<tr><td colspan="2" align="center">AMELIA</td></tr>
<tr><td align="right">Ah, you must leave me.</td><td align="right">Ah, mi lasciate ...</td></tr>
<tr><td>Do you see the wrong you're doing?</td><td>Son la vittima che geme,</td></tr>
<tr><td>You must save me, my reputation,</td><td>Il mio nome almen salvate,</td></tr>
<tr><td>or I die of shame and of horror,</td><td>O lo strazio ed il rossore</td></tr>
<tr><td>you must leave me or I will die.</td><td>La mia vita abbatterà.</td></tr>
</table>

<table>
<tr><td colspan="2" align="center">GUSTAVUS</td></tr>
<tr><td>Shall I leave you? No, no, never:</td><td>Io lasciarti? no, giammai;</td></tr>
<tr><td>no, I cannot, because I love you</td><td>Nol poss'io; ché m'arde in petto</td></tr>
<tr><td>with an everlasting passion.</td><td>Immortal di te l'affetto.</td></tr>
</table>

<table>
<tr><td colspan="2" align="center">AMELIA</td></tr>
<tr><td>Highness, for pity's sake, I beg ...</td><td>Conte, abbiatemi pietà.</td></tr>
</table>

<table>
<tr><td colspan="2" align="center">GUSTAVUS</td></tr>
<tr><td>Oh, believe that I adore you,</td><td>Così parli a chi t'adora?</td></tr>
<tr><td>every word is pleading for you.</td><td>Pietà chiedi, e tremi ancora?</td></tr>
<tr><td>Your fair name will be forever</td><td>Il tuo nome intemerato,</td></tr>
<tr><td>held in honour and in pride.</td><td>L'onor tuo sempre sarà.</td></tr>
</table>

<table>
<tr><td colspan="2" align="center">AMELIA</td></tr>
<tr><td>But Gustavus, I am married</td><td>Ma, Riccardo, io son d'altrui ...</td></tr>
<tr><td>to your faithful friend and comrade ...</td><td>Dell'amico più fidato ...</td></tr>
</table>

<table>
<tr><td colspan="2" align="center">GUSTAVUS</td></tr>
<tr><td>Dear Amelia!</td><td>Taci, Amelia!</td></tr>
</table>

<table>
<tr><td colspan="2" align="center">AMELIA</td></tr>
<tr><td align="right">I am the wife</td><td>[22]   Io son di lui,</td></tr>
<tr><td>of a man who would lay down his life
  for you.</td><td>Che daria la vita a te.</td></tr>
</table>

<table>
<tr><td colspan="2" align="center">GUSTAVUS</td></tr>
<tr><td>Cruel woman, still reminding me,</td><td>Ah crudele, e mel rammemori,</td></tr>
<tr><td>speaking words I would forget!</td><td>Lo ripeti innanzi a me!</td></tr>
<tr><td>Don't you know in my heart and my
  spirit</td><td>[23] Non sai tu che se l'anima mia</td></tr>
<tr><td>deep remorse comes to punish and chide
  me,</td><td>Il rimorso dilacera e rode,</td></tr>
<tr><td>yet there's something far deeper inside
  me,</td><td>Quel suo grido non cura, non ode,</td></tr>
<tr><td>the excitement and passion of love.</td><td>Sin che l'empie di fremiti amor?</td></tr>
<tr><td>Well I know I am yours and I swear it,</td><td>Non sai tu che di te resteria,</td></tr>
<tr><td>though my heart should stop beating
  and die!</td><td>Se cessasse di battere il cor!</td></tr>
<tr><td>Every night in a fever of longing,</td><td>Quante notti ho vegliato anelante!</td></tr>
<tr><td>I would struggle to conquer my
  weakness.</td><td>Come a lungo infelice lottai!</td></tr>
<tr><td>I would pray to my God and implore
  him</td><td>Quante volte dal cielo implorai</td></tr>
</table>

70

for the mercy that you ask of me!
But for this single moment I waited,
to my happiness you are the key.

La pietà che tu chiedi da me!
Ma per questo ho potuto un istante,
Infelice, non viver di te?

AMELIA

Ah, dearest Heaven I beg for compassion,
I must choose either death or dishonour;
Let the light of your mercy shine on her
who is straying and longs to be true.

Ah! Deh, soccorri tu, cielo, all'ambascia
Di chi sta tra l'infamia e la morte:
Tu pietoso rischiara le porte
Di salvezza all'errante mio piè.

to Gustavus

Leave me now; I'll not hear you, so leave me.
I am his, who would shed blood for you.

E tu va', ch'io non t'oda mi lascia;
Son di lui, che il suo sangue ti diè.

GUSTAVUS

I surrender life and kingdom
just to hear you . . .

La mia vita, l'universo,
Per un detto . . .

AMELIA

Heaven help me!   Ciel pietoso!

GUSTAVUS

Say you love me!   Di' che m'ami!

AMELIA

No, I cannot!   Va', Riccardo!

GUSTAVUS

Only tell me . . .   Un sol detto . . .

AMELIA

My heart, yes, I love you.   Ebben, sì, t'amo.

GUSTAVUS

Love me, Amelia!   M'ami, Amelia!

AMELIA

But my noble friend,   Ma tu, nobile,
help me conquer my own heart.   Me difendi dal mio cor!

GUSTAVUS
ecstatically

You love me, you love me! Oh, then let friendship,
let remorse forever vanish
from my heart: let all things perish,
all things go except for love.

M'ami, m'ami! oh, sia distrutto
Il rimorso, l'amicizia
Nel mio seno: estinto tutto,
Tutto sia fuorchè l'amor!

The sweetest glowing fire of love
is kindled here inside me:
to hold you here beside me
and hear the words you say!
Bright star, you shine in gloomy night,
my heart is yours forever:
make me as bright, then never
need the sun rise at dawning of day!

[24] Oh, qual soave brivido
L'acceso petto irrora!
Ah, ch'io t'ascolti ancora
Rispondermi così!
Astro di queste tenebre
A cui consacro il core,
Irradiami d'amore
E più non sorga il dì!

AMELIA

I dreamt a dream of horror,
to kill this love that masters me;
but still it grows in power,
it breaks my heart in two.
Will no firm hand awake me,
and show me some sweet remedy?

Ah, sul funereo letto
Ov'io sognava spegnerlo,
Gigante torna in petto
L'amor che mi ferì!
Chè non m'è dato in seno
A lui versar quest'anima?

71

If only death would take me,
I would find relief anew.

O nella morte almeno
Addormentarmi quì?

GUSTAVUS

Amelia! You love me, Amelia?
You love me?

Amelia! Tu m'ami, Amelia?
Tu m'ami?

AMELIA

Yes, I love you.

Sì, t'amo.

After the reprise of the duet, the moonlight grows brighter.

Scene and Terzetto.

AMELIA

What's that?

Ahimè!

listening

I hear a step!

S'appressa alcun!

GUSTAVUS

Not in this dark place of
death and desolation!

Chi giunge in questo
Soggiorno della morte?

He makes several steps.

Ah, yes, I see him . . .

Ah, non m'inganno!

Anckarstroem appears.

Your husband!

Renato!

AMELIA

Terrified, she lowers her veil.

Now Heaven help me!

Il mio consorte!

Scene Three. *Gustavus, Amelia and Anckarstroem.*

GUSTAVUS

You here?

Tu quì!

ANCKARSTROEM

Yes, to save you from men who are
hiding
up there; they are plotting.

Per salvarti da lor, che, celati

Lassù, t'hanno in mira.

GUSTAVUS

But why?

Chi son?

ANCKARSTROEM

They would kill you.

Congiurati.

AMELIA

O God!

O ciel!

ANCKARSTROEM

I passed by, my cloak wrapped around
me;

Trasvolai nel manto serrato,

they took me for one of their men in
the ambush.

Così che m'han preso per un dell'agguato,

Then one of their number was speaking:
'I saw him . . .

E intesi taluno proromper: 'L'ho visto:

Gustavus . . . a lady with him; she looked
like a stranger.'

È il Conte; un'ignota beltade è con esso.'

Said one of the others: 'A short-lived
attachment.

Poi altri qui volto: 'Fuggevole acquisto!

The dark grave awaits him; his tender
embraces

S'ei rade la fossa, se il tenero amplesso

are doomed to be cut short and that
very soon!'

Troncar di mia mano repente saprò!'

AMELIA
aside

How fearful!   Io muoio . . .

GUSTAVUS
to her

    Have courage.   Fa core.

ANCKARSTROEM
covering Gustavus with his cloak

    Now put on my cloak.   Ma questo ti do.
pointing out a little path to the right

Take care now, go this way, and you   E bada, lo scampo, t'è libero là.
  will escape.

GUSTAVUS
to Amelia, taking her by the hand

I have to protect you.   Salvarti degg'io . . .

AMELIA
softly, to him

    For heaven's sake, go!   Me misera! Va' . . .

ANCKARSTROEM
moving to Amelia

But you, fair young lady, would put   Ma voi non vorrete segnarlo, o signora,
  him in danger
if they saw you with him.   Al ferro spietato!

Anckarstroem goes to the back to see if anyone is approaching.

AMELIA
to Gustavus

    You must go without me!   Deh, solo t'invola.

GUSTAVUS

And leave you in danger?   Che qui t'abbandoni?

AMELIA

    Ah, make your escape   T'è libero ancora
while you can, go quickly!   Il passo, deh, fuggi . . .

GUSTAVUS

    All alone with him, how can   Lasciarti qui sola
I leave you? No, no, I'd much rather die!   Con esso? No, mai! piuttosto morrò!

AMELIA

Now leave, or this veil I will tear from   O fuggi, o che il velo dal capo torrò.
  my face.

GUSTAVUS

No, never.   Che dici?

AMELIA

    I mean it.   Risolvi.

GUSTAVUS

    I beg you.   Desisti.

AMELIA

    Farewell.   Lo vo'.
Gustavus hesitates, but she renews her command with a gesture.
to herself

Let Heaven protect him and spare him   Salvarlo a quest'alma se dato sarà.
  his life;
of bitter misfortune his heart knows   Del fiero suo fato più tema non ha.
  no fear.

73

When Anckarstroem reappears, the King goes to meet him.

GUSTAVUS
to Anckarstroem, solemnly

My dear friend, I ask for your help on your honour;
by the love that you bear me, give me your word.

Amico, gelosa t'affido una cura;
l'amor che mi porti, garante mi sta.

ANCKARSTROEM

You know you can trust me.

Affidati, imponi.

GUSTAVUS
indicating Amelia

This lady requires your protection and help: so give me your word ...
You must not address her or look in her face.

Promettimi, giura
Che tu l'addurrai, velata, in città,
Nè un detto, nè un guardo su essa trarrai.

ANCKARSTROEM

I swear it.

Lo giuro.

GUSTAVUS

At the gates of the city you go your own way and leave her.

E che tocche le porte, n'andrai
Da solo all'opposto.

ANCKARSTROEM

I swear it: have no fear.

Lo giuro, e sarà.

AMELIA
whispering to Gustavus, very agitated

Do you hear like a whispering in the dark,
the voices of death all around us?
Over there, from the dark, rocky hollow,
all your enemies coming this way?
They have taken an oath to destroy you ...
They are here to surround you and kill you ...
At your head they will strike and destroy you ...
Ah, I beg, go, and do not delay.

[25] Odi tu come fremono cupi
Per quest'aura gli accenti di morte?
Di lassù, da quei negri dirupi
Il segnal de' nemici partì.
Ne' lor petti scintillano d'ira ...

E già piomban, t'accerchiano fitti ...

Al tuo capo già volser la mira ...

Per pietà, va', t'invola di qui.

ANCKARSTROEM
emerging from the back, where he has been looking around

You must go, you must go, on the path
I hear them tracking you nearer and nearer.
They have taken an oath not to fear you,
but to topple you down from your throne.
Save yourself while the way is still open,
you must fly or your enemies trap you:
save yourself for the sake of your people,
for your life is a part of their own.

Fuggi, fuggi: per l'orrida via
Sento l'orma de' passi spietati;

Allo scambio dei detti esecrati

Ogni destra la daga brandì.

Va', ti salva, o che il varco all'uscita
Qui fra poco serrarsi vedrai;
Va', ti salva; del popolo è vita
Questa vita che getti così.

GUSTAVUS

All the traitors have banded together:
are they coming to trap and to kill me?
Ah! But I am the one who is guilty,

Traditor, congiurarti son essi
Che minacciano il viver mio?
Ah, l'amico ho tradito pur io ...

by betraying the love of his heart.
I would like to defy them and stay,
but my guilty love makes me a coward.
May the mercy of Heaven, I pray,
now enfold her and keep her from
  harm.

Son colui che nel cor lo feri.
Innocente, sfidati li avrei:
Or d'amore colpevole . . . fuggo.
La pietà del Signore su lei
Posi l'ale, protegga i suoi dì!

Exit Gustavus.

Scene Four. *Anckarstroem and Amelia. Then Ribbing and Horn.*

Scene, Chorus and Quartet. Second Finale.

ANCKARSTROEM
Come, follow me.   Seguitemi.

AMELIA
Dear Heaven!   Mio Dio!

ANCKARSTROEM
    Why are you trembling?   Perchè tremate?
There is nothing to fear. I am your   Fida scorte vi son, l'amico accento
  friend:
I will keep you safe from harm.   Vi risollevi il cor!

Scene Five. *Ribbing, Horn and their followers.*

AMELIA
    Here they are!   Eccoli!

ANCKARSTROEM
    Hurry,   Presto,
take hold of my arm.   Appoggiatevi a me.

AMELIA
    I feel I'm dying.   Morir mi sento.

CONSPIRATORS
in the distance

Now we have him at our mercy,   Accentiamoci su lui,
his last hour is gone for ever.   Chè scoccata è l'ultim'ora.
When the morning sun has risen,   Il saluto dell'aurora
it will shine upon a corpse.   Pel cadavere sarà.

RIBBING
Do you see the white veil gleaming,   Scerni tu quel bianco velo
picking out his latest goddess?   Onde spicca la sua dea?

HORN
We shall pluck him down from Heaven   Si precipiti dal cielo
to Hades.   All'inferno.

ANCKARSTROEM
in a loud voice

    Who is there?   Chi va là?

RIBBING
That's not his voice!   Non è desso!

HORN
    It's not Gustavus!   O furor mio!

CONSPIRATORS
Not Gustavus!   Non è il Conte!

ANCKARSTROEM
    No, it is I,   No, son io,
not the King who stands before you   Che dinanzi a voi qui sta.
  here.

75

HORN
mocking

How surprising!   Il suo fido!

RIBBING

      Well, it seems   Men di voi
that you had better luck than we did: Fortunati fummo noi;
in the dark a lovely lady,   Chè il sorriso d'una bella
full of smiles and tender grace?   Stemmo indarno ad aspettar.

HORN

May we also be rewarded?   Io per altro voltto ameno
May we see the lady's face?   Vo' a quest'Iside mirar!

Some of the conspirators return with burning torches.

ANCKARSTROEM
with his hand on his sword

I forbid it: if you move,   Non un passo: se l'osate
you'll have to fight me . . .   Traggo il ferro . . .

RIBBING

      Are you serious?   Minacciate?

HORN

Let him fight us.   Non vi temo.

The moon shines in all its glory.

AMELIA

   ·   Oh, Heaven help me!   O ciel, alta!

CONSPIRATORS
to Anckarstroem

Put your sword up.   Giù l'acciaro . . .

ANCKARSTROEM

      You are traitors.   Traditori!

HORN
going to tear the veil from Amelia

Take the veil off!   Vo' finirla . . .

ANCKARSTROEM
unsheathing his sword

      Now if you touch her   E la tua vita
you will answer with your life. Quest'insulto pagherà.

As they all lunge towards Anckarstroem, Amelia, beside herself and trembling, lets fall the veil.

AMELIA

No: you must not . . .   No; fermatevi . . .

ANCKARSTROEM
thunderstruck

      Ah! . . . Amelia!   Che! . . . Amelia!

RIBBING, HORN AND THE CONSPIRATORS

No! His wife! His own wife!   Lei! Sua moglie! Sua moglie!

AMELIA

      Oh God! Forgive!   O ciel! pietà!

ANCKARSTROEM
trembling

Amelia!   Amelia!

Can I be dreaming? Strange assignation:
the husband chooses a new sensation.
Here in the moonlight, as dew is falling,
we find him making love to his own
wife. Ha! Ha! Ha!
A piece of gossip to spread around,
a charming story for all the town.

[26] Ve', se di notte qui colla sposa
L'innamorato campion si posa
E come al raggio lunar del miele
Sulle rugiade corcar si sa! Ah! Ah! Ah!

[27] E che baccano sul caso strano
E che commenti per la città.

CONSPIRATORS

See how the drama turns into laughter.
[How very delightful!] Ha! Ha! Ha! Ha!

Ve', la tragedia mutò in commedia.
[Piace volissima]*, Ah! Ah! Ah! Ah!

AMELIA

Ah, who will help you, and show you pity,
forlorn Amelia, have you no friend?
You lie here weeping, in shame and
sorrow,
but is there no one to dry your tears?

A chi nel mondo crudel più mai,
Misera Amelia, ti volgerai? ...
La tua spregiata lacrima, quale,

Qual man pietosa rasciugherà.

ANCKARSTROEM
gazing at the path by which Gustavus left

I come to save him, and he rewards me:
he stains my lady with black dishonour.
The friend I trusted, whom I would die
for:
he breaks my heart and wrecks my life.

Così mi paga se l'ho salvato!
Ei m'ha la donna contaminato!
Per lui non posso levar la fronte,

Sbranato il core per sempre m'ha!

approaching Ribbing and Horn, and in a determined voice

May I ask you both to meet me
at my house tomorrow morning?

Converreste in casa mia
Sul mattino di domani?

RIBBING AND HORN

Shall we come to beg forgiveness?

Forse ammenda aver chiedete?

ANCKARSTROEM

No, I've something else in mind.

No, ben altro in cor mi sta.

RIBBING AND HORN

What can it be?

Che vi punge?

ANCKARSTROEM

     Come tomorrow,
I will tell you.

     Lo saprete,
Se verrete.

RIBBING AND HORN

  We will be there.

E ci vedrai.

as they leave, with their followers

Let us go and be careful,
take a different road at parting.
In the morning we'll be smarting
from the great things in his mind.

Dunque andiam: per vie diverse
L'un dall'altro s'allontani!
Il mattino di domani
Grandi cose apprenderà.

RIBBING AND HORN

This way.
See how the drama turns into laughter.
Ha! Ha! Ha!
A piece of gossip to spread around,
a charming story for all the town.

Andiam.
Ve', la tragedia mutò in commedia.
Ah! Ah! Ah!
[27] E che baccano sul caso strano
E che commenti per la città.

This verse is repeated by a few of the Chorus a long way off.

---

* For a discussion of why this was never set to music, see Powers, p. 32 *et seq.*

ANCKARSTROEM

remaining alone with Amelia, addressing her with a shudder

I have sworn that I will take you	Ho giurato che alle porte
to the town and there we will part.	V'addurrei della città.

AMELIA

to herself

In his voice there is no pity,	Come sonito di morte
how it strikes me to the heart.	La sua voce al cor mi va!

ANCKARSTROEM

Come on! Come on!	Andiam! Andiam!

AMELIA

Ah no! I beg!	Ah no! pietà.

They leave by the small path. The conspirators continue singing off stage.

The curtain falls quickly.

Birgit Nilsson as Amelia and Erik Saeden as her husband, Count Holberg (ie. Renato), with the Royal Swedish Opera on a visit to Covent Garden in 1960 (photo: Donald Southern/Royal Opera House Archives)

Act Three

Scene One. *A study in Anckarstroem's house. Two bronze vases stand on a small fireplace at the side; opposite is a bookcase. At the back, there is a magnificent full-length portrait of Gustavus and, in the middle of the stage, there is a table. Enter Anckarstroem and Amelia.*

Scene and Aria.

ANCKARSTROEM
putting down his sword, and closing the door

Such a crime is past forgiving.	A tal colpa è nulla il pianto,
Tears won't clear it nor excuse it.	Non la terge e non la scusa.
Every oath would be a lie;	Ogni prece è vana omai;
I'll have vengeance, you shall die.	Sangue vuolsi, e tu morrai.

AMELIA

If I'm guilty, then do me justice;	Ma se reo, se reo soltanto
show me proof that I am guilty ...	È l'indizio che m'accusa?

ANCKARSTROEM

Vile adulteress.	Taci, adultera.

AMELIA

Great Heaven!	Gran Dio!

ANCKARSTROEM

Pray that God may grant you mercy.	Chiedi a lui misericordia.

AMELIA

Will you judge me on suspicion?	E ti basta un sol sospetto?
All you want is blood and vengeance?	E vuoi dunque il sangue mio?
You would shame me and deny me	E m'infami, e più non senti
simple justice, simple truth?	Né giustizia, né pietà?

ANCKARSTROEM

I'll have vengeance. You shall die.	Sangue volse. Tu morrai.

AMELIA

For a moment I felt love,	Un istante, è ver, l'amai,
but I never soiled your name.	Ma il tuo nome non macchiai.
God knows well that I have never	Sallo Iddio, che nel mio petto
known a love that was unworthy.	Mai non arse indegno affetto.

ANCKARSTROEM
picking up his sword again

Have you finished? Dare you lie?	Hai finito! è tardi omai ...
I'll have vengeance, you shall die.	Sangue vuolsi, e tu morrai.

AMELIA

Ah! I'm fainting! ... So be it ... grant me	Ah! Mi sveni! ... ebbene, sia ...
one last favour ...	Ma una grazia ...

ANCKARSTROEM

Not from me.	Non a me.
Turn your prayers to God in Heaven.	La tua prece al ciel rivolgi.

AMELIA
kneeling

Just one final word to you.	Solo un detto ancora a te.
Hear me, it will be the last.	M'odi, l'ultimo sarà.
I'll die, but first I beg you,	[28] Morrò, ma prima in grazia,
grant me, in mercy, a favour:	Deh! mi consenti almeno

let me embrace my son,	L'unico figlio mio
kiss him goodbye for ever.	Avvincere al mio seno.
If to a wife you say no	E se alla moglie nieghi
to this my last request,	Quest'ultimo favor,
do not deny the prayer	Non rifiutarlo ai prieghi
from a fond mother's breast.	Del mio materno cor.
I'll die, but you must promise me,	Morrò, ma queste viscere
to let his kiss console me,	Consolino i suoi baci,
so as my life is ending,	Or che l'estrema è giunta
his loving arms will enfold me.	Dell'ore mie fugaci ...
Seeing his father pitiless,	Spenta per man del padre,
he will stretch out his hand	La man ei stenderà
to bless his loving mother;	Sugli occhi d'una madre
he will see her no more.	Che mai più non vedrà!

Scene and Aria.

ANCKARSTROEM

gesturing towards a door, without looking up

Stand up! If you wish it,	Alzati! là tuo figlio
I give you leave to see your son.	A te concedo riveder. Nell'ombra
In darkness and in silence go,	E nel silenzio, là,
and try to hide your shame and my dishonour.	Il tuo rossor e l'onta mia nascondi.

Exit Amelia.

It is not her, with her frail	Non è su lei, nel suo
woman's feelings that I mean to punish.	Fragile petto che colpir degg'io.
Another ... blood from a traitor	Altro, ben altro sangue a terger dèssi
to wash my soul clean for ever ...	L'offesa ...

staring at the portrait

It is Gustavus!	Il sangue tuo!
Now with my sword I'll draw blood,	E lo trarrà il pugnale
treacherous friend and master:	Dallo sleal tuo core,
for the wrong you have done me,	Delle lagrime mie vendicator,
I'll have revenge!	vendicator!

It was you who ensnared and defiled my love,	[29] Eri tu che macchiavi quell'anima,
the perfection of all that I lived for ...	La delizia dell'anima mia;
You, my brother, with one terrible treachery,	Che m'affidi e d'un tratto esecrabile
life and love you have poisoned for me.	L'universo avveleni per me!
To betray is your way of rewarding	Traditor! Che compensi in tal guisa
the dear friend who was closest to you.	Dell'amico tuo primo la fe'!
Oh, the joy of my life lost for ever,	[30] O dolcezze perdute! O memorie
sweet embraces that raised me to Heaven,	D'un amplesso che l'essere india!
when Amelia so lovely, so innocent,	Quando Amelia sì bella, sì candida
lay beside me and gave me her love.	Sul mio seno brillava d'amor!
All is over: and nothing is left me, but hatred	È finita, non siede che l'odio
and death in my sad widowed heart.	E la morte nel vedovo cor!

Scene Two. *Anckarstroem; Ribbing and Horn enter, greeting him coldly.*

The Oath, Terzetto and Quartet.

ANCKARSTROEM

We're alone here. Now listen. I have discovered	Siam soli. Udite. Ogni disegno vostro

what you are plotting. You are conspiring to murder Gustavus.

M'è noto. Voi di Riccardo la morte Volete.

HORN

You're dreaming!

È un sogno!

ANCKARSTROEM
showing them some papers on the table

These papers prove it!

Ho qui le prove!

RIBBING
trembling

And now you have got them you'll show them to the King?

Ed ora La trama al Conte svelerai?

ANCKARSTROEM

No: I want To join you.

No: voglio Dividerla.

RIBBING AND HORN

You're joking.

Tu scherzi.

ANCKARSTROEM

Not by words, but by my actions I'll allay your suspicions.
I'm one of you now, so take me and trust me.
I will welcome this bloody adventure: take my young son as hostage. You can kill him if I fail you.

E non co' detti: Ma qui col fatto struggerò i sospetti.
Io son vostro, compagno m'avrete
Senza posa a quest'opra di sangue: Arra il figlio vi sia. L'uccidete Se vi manco.

RIBBING

This change in your feelings is so strange to those who know you.

Ma tal mutamento È credibile appena.

ANCKARSTROEM

Don't bother to ask for a reason. I'm yours now, and the life of my only son as hostage!

Qual fu La cagion non cercate. Son vostro Per la vita dell'unico figlio!

RIBBING

Is he lying?

Ei non mente?

HORN

No, he means it.

Ei non mente.

ANCKARSTROEM

Do you doubt me?

Esitate?

RIBBING AND HORN

No more.

Non più.

ANCKARSTROEM, RIBBING AND HORN

No more.

Non più.

Let the shame we have suffered unite us, one in heart, one in vengeance for all. Let our anger devour and ignite us, on that criminal's head let it fall.

[31] Dunque l'onta di tutti sol una, Una il cor, la vendetta sarà, Che tremenda, repente, digiuna Su quel capo esecrato cadrà!

ANCKARSTROEM

I've a favour to ask of you.

D'una grazia vi supplico.

RIBBING

What is it?

E quale?

81

ANCKARSTROEM

That the dagger that strikes him be mine.

Che sia dato d'ucciderlo a me.

RIBBING

That is my right: my lands and my castle
he has stolen. I hope to destroy him.

No, Renato: l'avito castello
A me tolse, e tal dritto a me spetta.

HORN

What of me whom he robbed of a brother?
Waiting ten years in aching need for vengeance,
I have lived in a torment;
you cannot deny me.

Ed a me cui spegneva il fratello,
Cui decenne agonia di vendetta
Senza requie divora, qual parte
Assegnate?

ANCKARSTROEM

Control yourself:
let us draw lots so that Fate can decide.

Chetatevi, solo
Qui la sorte decidere de'.

He takes a vase from the chimneypiece and places it on the table. Ribbing writes three names on pieces of paper, and throws them into it.

Scene Three. *Amelia and the same.*

ANCKARSTROEM

Who is there?

E chi vien?

meeting Amelia as she enters

You?

Tu?

AMELIA

Young Oscar is here
with a note from His Highness.

V'è Oscar che porta
Un invito del Conte.

ANCKARSTROEM
shuddering

From him? . . .
We are busy. You remain here with us:
maybe Heaven has brought you to help us.

Di lui? . . .
Che m'aspetti. E tu resta, lo dei,
Poichè parmi che il cielo t'ha scorta.

AMELIA
to herself

Ah, what terror and grief overwhelm me!
Ah, their menacing glances repel me!

Qual tristezza m'assale, qual pena!
Qual terribile lampo balena!

ANCKARSTROEM
indicating his wife to Ribbing and Horn

Do not fear: she knows nothing. My wife's
coming here is a most happy omen.

Nulla sa: non temete. Costei
Esser debbe anzi l'auspice lieto.

to Amelia, pulling her to the table

There are three names inside here.
Yours shall be
the innocent hand to choose one.

V'han tre nomi in quell'urna: un ne tragga
L'innocente tua mano.

AMELIA
trembling

Tell me why?

E perchè?

ANCKARSTROEM
with a thunderous look in his eyes

Just obey me: and ask nothing more.

Ubbidisci: non chieder di più.

82

AMELIA
aside

I am certain that this barbarous order makes me a partner in bloodshed and murder.	Non v'è dubbio; il feroce decreto Mi vuol parte ad un'opra di sangue.

Shuddering, Amelia slowly approaches the table where the vase has been placed. Anckarstroem watches her all the time with eyes blazing; finally on the ppp in the orchestra, Amelia, with trembling hand, takes out one of the pieces of paper, which her husband then hands to Ribbing.

ANCKARSTROEM

Say the name Fate has chosen.	Qual è dunque l'eletto?

RIBBING
bitterly

Anckarstroem.	Renato.

ANCKARSTROEM
with exaltation

I am chosen! There is justice in Heaven;	Il mio nome! O giustizia del fato;

trembling with joy

sweetest vengeance forever is mine!	La vendetta mi deleghi tu!

AMELIA
aside

They are plotting his death, I can feel it! And they make no attempt to conceal it! Soon their weapons will glitter in hatred as they rain down their blows on his head!	Ah! del Conte la morte si vuole! Nol celar le crudeli parole! Su quel campo snudati dall'ira I lor ferri scintillano già.

ANCKARSTROEM, RIBBING AND HORN

He shall pay for the wrongs of our country, he who lied when he boasted of loyalty. He did murder, and he shall be murdered: just reward for his crimes is his due.	Sconterà dell'America il pianto Lo sleal che ne fece suo vanto. Se trafisse, soccomba trafitto, Tal mercede pagata gli va!

AMELIA

They are plotting his death, I can feel it! Ah, save him . . . That is what I must do!	Ah! del Conte la morte si vuole! I ferri scintillano già!

Scene and Quintet.

ANCKARSTROEM
to the door

Let the messenger enter.	Il messagio entri.

OSCAR
to Amelia

I am bidden by His Highness to invite you, you and your husband, to a ball this very evening.	Alle danze Questa sera, se gradite, Con lo sposo, il mio signore Vi desidera . . .

AMELIA
distressed

I cannot.	Nol posso.

ANCKARSTROEM

Will the King be there himself?	Anche il Conte vi sarà?

OSCAR

Surely.

Certo.

RIBBING AND HORN
to themselves

What fortune!

Oh sorte!

ANCKARSTROEM
to the page, but looking at his companions

His invitation
does us honour.

Tanto invito
So che valga.

OSCAR

It is a masked ball,
brilliant as possible.

È un ballo in maschera
splendidissimo.

ANCKARSTROEM

That's excellent!

Benissimo!

pointing to Amelia

I and my wife will both be there.

Ella meco interverrà.

AMELIA

Great Heavens!

Gran Dio!

RIBBING AND HORN
aside

The disguise will make it easier
for us all to strike the blow.

E noi pur, se da quell'abito
Più spedito il colpo va.

OSCAR

On every floor the music plays
and lights are bright and blazing,
where all the city's youth and beauty
seem evermore amazing:
they come to dance, they come to sing,
from near and far!

[32] Di che fulgor, che musiche
Esulteran le soglie,
Ove di tante giovani
Bellezze il fior s'accoglie,
Di quante altrice palpita
Questa gentil città!

AMELIA
to herself

And mine the hand that drew his name,
and joined me to their faction:
so my choice made me accomplice to
my husband's action.
That noble heart will die today
under a fatal star.

Ed io medesma, io misera,
Lo scritto inesorato
Trassi dall'urna complice,
Pel mio consorte irato:
Su cui del cor più nobile
Ferma la morte sta.

ANCKARSTROEM
aside

There where the dancers weave their
way,
my mind can see the picture,
his blood I see it staining the
palace floor in tincture;
no word of pity spoken,
no word my joy to mar.

Là fra le danze esanime

La mente mia sel pinge . . .
Ove del proprio sangue
Il pavimento tinge.
Spira dator d'infamie
Senza trovar pietà.

RIBBING AND HORN
between themselves

This dance will bring us sweet revenge,
now no man will deter us.
In all the merry masquerade,
disguise will serve our purpose:
the ball will be a funeral,
where pallid phantoms are.

Una vendetta in domino
È ciò che torna all'uopo.
Fra l'urto delle maschere
Non fallirà lo scopo;
Sarà una danza funebre
Con pallide beltà.

AMELIA

to herself

I must send him a warning but I can't betray my husband ...	Prevenirlo potessi, e non tradire Lo sposo mio!

OSCAR

And you will be our queen for the evening.	Reina Della festa sarete.

AMELIA

to herself

The fortune-teller Arvidson!	Forse potrallo Ulrica.

Anckarstroem, Ribbing and Horn speak rapidly and quietly to each other as they leave.

RIBBING AND HORN

What kind of costume shall we wear?	E qual costume indosserem?

ANCKARSTROEM

Our coats should be blue — a sash upon our left side like this, entwined with scarlet ribbons.	Azzurra La veste e da vermiglio Nastro le ciarpe al manco lato attorte.

RIBBING AND HORN

We must agree upon a password.	E qual accento a ravvisarci?

ANCKARSTROEM

Vengeance!	Morte!

Scene Five. *A sumptuous, small apartment of the King. A table with writing materials; at the back is a great curtain which will be drawn aside to reveal the ball.*

Third Finale. Scene and Romanza.

GUSTAVUS

alone

Surely she's safe at home now: God grant her peace. Our honour and our duty come between us and part us forever. And now, Anckarstroem is appointed to Finland ... and his Amelia will go there too. No final parting: the water and land will divide us ... My heart be silent.	Forse la soglia attinse, E posa alfin. L'onore Ed il dover fra i nostri petti han rotto L'abisso. Ah, sì, Renato Rivedrà l'Inghilterra* ... e la sua sposa Lo seguirà. Senza un addio, l'immenso Oceàn ne separi ... e taccia il core.

He writes, and at the moment when he is about to add his signature, he lets the pen drop.

Must it be so? Oh God, show me my duty.	Esito ancor? ma, oh ciel, non lo degg'io?

He signs the paper, and puts it in his breast-pocket.

Ah! I have signed it: my sacrifice of feeling!	Ah, l'ho segnato il sacrifizio mio!

Your light that shone so fair on me is clouded now forever, and yet the bond our love has made no power on earth will sever. Always your precious memory is treasured in my heart.	[33]	Ma se m'è forza perderti Per sempre, o luce mia, A te verrà il mio palpito Sotto qual ciel tu sia. Chiusa la tua memoria Nell'intimo del cor.

sombrely

But now what fearful warning is growing here inside me?	Ed or qual reo presagio Lo spirito m'assale,

---

* Lit. 'Renato' will see England again.

Does it foretell our meeting,	Che il rivederti annunzia
destiny come to guide me . . .	Quasi un desio fatale . . .
marking our final hour of love,	Come se fosse l'ultima
final for we must part?	Ora del nostro amor?

Dance music is heard from within. Festive dancing and chorus [34]

Ah! She is there . . . and I could see her . . . and maybe	Ah! dessa è là . . . potrei vederla . . . ancora
I could speak just a word . . .	Riparlarle potrei . . .
But no: now everything tears us apart.	Ma no: ché tutto or mi strappa da lei.

Scene Six. *Enter Oscar, a paper in his hand.*

OSCAR

I bring a letter from a strange young lady.	Ignota donna questo foglio diemmi.
'For His Highness', she whispered. 'Be sure that	E pel Conte, diss'ella; a lui lo reca
no one else is with him.'	E di celato.

Gustavus reads the paper.

GUSTAVUS
having read it

'At the ball an attempt	Che nel ballo alcuno
will be made on your life: be careful.'	Alla mia vita attenterà, sta detto.
But if I don't go,	Ma se m'arresto,
they will say I'm afraid. No, no: I won't have	Ch'io pavento diran. Nol vo': nessuno
them think that I'm afraid. You go: get ready,	Pur sospettarlo de'. Tu va': t'appresta,
and hurry, share in the joys of the evening.	E ratto, per gioir meco alla festa.

Exit Oscar. Gustavus remains alone, and breaks out violently:

Yes, I will see Amelia,	Sì, rivederti Amelia,
glowing in beauty there.	E nella tua beltà,
Ah, once again my tender heart	Anco una volta l'anima
will be on fire with love!	D'amor mi brillerà.

Scene Seven. *A splendid and spacious ballroom, brilliantly illuminated and decorated for a ball. There is festive music before the dances and even as the curtain rises the stage is filled with guests. The majority are masked, some in domino, others in gala costumes with uncovered faces; there are some young creoles among the dancing couples. Some pursue, others escape; some pay their respects, while others are more forward in their behaviour. There are negro servants, and all breathes of magnificence and high spirits.* [34]

GENERAL CHORUS

What ecstasy in dancing	Fervono amori e danze
and smiles of lovers glancing,	Nelle felici stanze,
to show that life is pleasure,	Onde la vita è solo
a dream of pleasure passing.	Un sogno lusinghier.
Night full of precious moments,	Notte de' cari istanti,
of breathless joys and torments,	De' palpiti e de' canti,
oh, let it last forever,	Perchè non fermi, 'l volo
forever let it last!	Sull'onda del piacer?

Scene Eight. *Ribbing, Horn and their followers enter in blue dominoes, with scarlet sashes. Anckarstroem, in the same costume, slowly approaches them.*

RIBBING
indicating Anckarstroem to Horn

One of our friends approaches.	Altro de' nostri è questo.

Vengeance!   Morte!

ANCKARSTROEM
bitterly
Yes: vengeance!   Sì: morte!
He will not come.   Ma non verrà.

RIBBING AND HORN
You mean it?   Che parli?

ANCKARSTROEM
Waiting like this is useless.   Qui l'aspettarlo è vano.

RIBBING
Really?   Come?

HORN
But why?   Perchè?

ANCKARSTROEM
Well, maybe he had a warning.   Vi basti saperlo altrove.

RIBBING
We really are   O sorte
unlucky!   Ingannitrice!

HORN
trembling with fury
He's always slipping through our fingers.   Sempre ne sfuggirà di mano!

ANCKARSTROEM
Don't talk so loud; there's someone   Parlate basso: alcuno lo sguardo a noi
who's watching us, I'm sure.   fermò.

RIBBING
But who?   E chi?

ANCKARSTROEM
There to the left in the cloak of black   Quello a sinistra dal breve domino.
and white.

They disperse, but Anckarstroem is followed by Oscar, who is masked.

OSCAR
to Anckarstroem
Surely I know you behind the mask?   Più non ti lascio, o maschera;
You can't deceive me.   mal ti nascondi.

ANCKARSTROEM
drawing back
Be off now!   Eh via!

OSCAR
still following him; with vivacity
Yes, you are Anckarstroem.   Tu se' Renato.

ANCKARSTROEM
pulling off Oscar's mask
And Oscar I see.   E Oscar tu sei.

OSCAR
You shouldn't do that!   Qual villania!

ANCKARSTROEM
Oh really? A very odd way to do your   Ma bravo, e ti par dunque convenienza
duty: questa

to leave your master sleeping and slip
off to the party?

Che mentre il Conte dorme, tu scivoli
alla festa?

OSCAR

The King is here . . .

Il Conte è qui . . .

ANCKARSTROEM
starting

What? Show me.

Che! dove?

OSCAR

I've told you.

L'ho detto . . .

ANCKARSTROM

All right . . . but where?

Ebben! . . . qual è?

OSCAR

I will not tell.

Non vel dirò!

ANCKARSTROEM

A secret!

Gran cosa?

OSCAR
turning his back
Go seek him out yourself.

Cercatelo da voi.

ANCKARSTROEM
in a friendly manner
Be good!

Orsù!

OSCAR

If I'm to betray him, I'll ask a big
reward.

E per fargli il tiro che regalaste a me?

ANCKARSTROEM

You ask too much; tell me only what
costume he is in?

Via calmati: almen dirmi del suo costume
puoi?

Canzone

OSCAR
playfully

Betray his secret?
No, no, I'll keep it,
for I am bidden
to keep it hidden.
I know full well,
but I'll not tell.
Tra, la, la, la,
la, la, la, la.
A love so deep
my heart will keep,
though Oscar knows it,
he won't disclose it.
He will not sell,
he must not tell.
tra, la, la, la,
la, la, la, la.

[35] Saper vorreste,
Di che si veste,
Quando l'è cosa
Ch'ei vuol nascosa.
Oscar lo sa,
Ma nol dirà.
Tra, là, là, là,
Là, là, là, là.
Pieno d'amore
Mi balza il core,
Ma pur discreto.
Serba il secreto.
Nol rapirà
Grado o beltà.
Tra, là, là, là,
Là, là, là, là.

At this moment, groups of maskers and dancing couples cross the front of the stage and separate the
page from Anckarstroem. Reprise of the chorus. They return upstage, and disappear at the back.

ANCKARSTROEM
catching up with him again
Surely you know the man he values as
his friend?

So che tu sai distinguere gli amici suoi?

OSCAR

You're going to surprise him, and maybe you'd like to play a joke?

V'alletta Interrogarlo, e forse celiar con esso un po'?

ANCKARSTROEM

Precisely.

Appunto.

OSCAR

And then you'd get me into trouble with His Highness?

E compromettere di poi chi ve l'ha detta?

ANCKARSTROEM

Of course not. It's confidential; I have to let him know.

M'offendi. È confidenza che quanto importi io so.

OSCAR

You push so hard . . .

Vi preme assai . . .

ANCKARSTROEM

I have to tell him something important, before the ball is over: give me your help. If you refuse, it may be serious, and you will be the culprit.

Degg'io di gravi cose ad esso, Pria che la notte inoltri, qui favellar. Su te Farò cader la colpa, se non mi fia concesso.

OSCAR

Well then . . .

Dunque . . .

ANCKARSTROEM

It is for him I ask it, and not for me.

Fai grazia a lui, se parli, e non a me.

OSCAR
coming closer, and quickly

Cloak long and black, a rose-coloured ribbon on his shoulder.

Veste una cappa nera, con roseo nastro al petto.

He is about to move away.

ANCKARSTROEM

And tell me something further.

Una parola ancora.

OSCAR
disappearing in the crowd

I've said too much already.

Più che abbastanza ho detto.

Dancers cross the stage; Anckarstroem sees one of his men in the distance, and disappears in that direction. A little later Gustavus, emerging from among the couples at the back, comes forward looking thoughtful. He wears a black domino with a red ribbon, and behind him follows Amelia in a white domino.

Reprise of the chorus. [34] *Scene and Duet.* [36]

AMELIA
quietly, so as not to be recognised

Ah! Are you mad? I warned you . . .

Ah! perché qui! fuggite . . .

GUSTAVUS

I thank you for your letter.

Sei quella dello scritto?

AMELIA

Your enemies will kill you.

La morte qui v'accerchia . . .

GUSTAVUS

I'm not a coward, I won't run away.

Non penetra nel mio Petto il terror.

AMELIA

Go quickly, go quickly, save yourself quickly

Fuggite, fuggite, o che trafitto

89

or you will die.   Cadrete qui!

GUSTAVUS

I have to know: tell me, who are you?   Rivelami il nome tuo.

AMELIA

Great Heaven,   Gran Dio!
I cannot.   Nol posso.

GUSTAVUS

Then why this weeping . . . imploring me   E perchè piangi . . . mi supplichi atterrita?
  in terror?
You seem to feel such pity, why is my life   Onde cotanta senti pietà della mia vita?
  important?

AMELIA

between sobs which reveal her true voice

If it would save you, I would give my   Tutto per essa, tutto il sangue mio darei!
  heart's blood for you.

GUSTAVUS

I know your voice, Amelia: my angel   In van ti celi, Amelia: quell'angelo tu
  here beside me.   sei!

AMELIA

in despair

I love you, I love you more than life.   T'amo, sì, t'amo, e in lagrime
Ah, how can I persuade you?   A' piedi tuoi m'atterro,
Hear me, they plan to murder you: Ove t'anela incognito
friends whom you trust betrayed you.   Della vendetta il ferro.
Your bloodstained corpse tomorrow   Cadavere domani
we'll mourn in endless sorrow.   Sarai se qui rimani:
save yourself, go, forget me,   Salvati, va', mi lascia,
leave me, and fly from their hate.   Fuggi dall'odio lor.

GUSTAVUS

Sure of your love, Amelia,   [37] Sin che tu m'ami, Amelia,
no care can come to grieve me: Non curo il fato mio,
you are the breath of life to me,   Non ho che te nell'anima,
grace can never leave me.   E l'universo obblio.
I fear my death no longer,   Nè so temer la morte,
the power inside me is stronger;   Perchè di lei più forte
a radiance that inspires me,   È l'aura che m'inebria
this pure and heavenly love.   Del tuo divino amor.

AMELIA

Save yourself. Go. Save yourself.   Salvati. Va. Salvati.
Surely you do not wish   Dunque vedermi vuoi
to see me die in shame and sorrow?   D'affanno morta e di vergogna?

GUSTAVUS

You will   Salva
be safe. Tomorrow, with your husband,   Ti vo'. Domani con Renato andrai . . .
  you go . . .

AMELIA

Go where?   Dove?

GUSTAVUS*

. . . on a mission to Finland.   . . . Al natio tuo cielo.

---

* Lit. 'Riccardo' sends 'Renato' and 'Amelia' to their native skies, ie England, which is odd if
Renato is a 'Creole' in the sense that he was born in America, even if he is not half-
caste.

AMELIA

We go to Finland?   In Inghilterra?

GUSTAVUS

It breaks my heart ... and yet it must
be ... you have to go.

Mi schianto il cor ... ma partirai ...
ma ... addio.

AMELIA

Gustavus!   Riccardo!

GUSTAVUS

He tears himself away from her, but after a few steps he turns to her and says with all his soul:
Amelia: never to hold you or see you.   Amelia: anco una volta addio.

AMELIA

Oh God!   Ohimè!

GUSTAVUS

Never to hold you or see you!
Forever!

L'ultima volta addio!
Addio!

ANCKARSTROEM

unobserved, he suddenly throws himself between them, and stabs Gustavus
May you be damned forever!   E tu ricevi il mio!

GUSTAVUS

Oh God!   Ahimè!

AMELIA

with a scream

Oh, help him!   Soccorso!

OSCAR

running up to him

Dear God! The King has been murdered!   Oh ciel! Ei trucidato!

From all sides come ladies, officials and guards.

SOME CHORUS

The King?   Da chi?

OTHERS

Where is the killer?   Ov'è l'infame?

Ribbing and Horn appear at the back.

OSCAR

pointing at Anckarstroem
Here he is!   Eccol!

All surround him and take off their masks.

ALL

It can't be!   Renato!

Ah! Kill him, the monster,
the murderer, he must die!
Destroy him and punish him
and crucify!

[38] Ah! Morte, infamia
Sul taditor!
L'acciar lo laceri
Vendicator!

GUSTAVUS

No, no ... No harm to him ...
I order it.

No, no ... lasciate lo ...
Lasciate lo.

to Anckarstroem; touching the despatch, he gestures him to approach
You ... hear my words.   Tu ... m'odi ancor.

Final scene.
She is blameless: as I am dying
I swear it, may God be my witness.

Ella è pura: in braccio a morte
Te lo giuro, Iddio m'ascolta:

91

Final scene.

She is blameless: as I am dying
I swear it, may God be my witness.
Hear me now: I loved Amelia
like a goddess, a star apart.

Ella è pura: in braccio a morte
Te lo giuro, Iddio m'ascolta:
Io che amai la tua consorte,
Rispettato ho il suo candor,

He hands over the despatch.

I had ordered a new appointment,
you and she were soon to leave me ...
Though I loved, there was no blemish
on your name or her pure heart.

A novello incarco asceso
Tu con lei partir dovevi ...
Io l'amai, ma volli illeso
Il tuo nome ed il suo cor!

AMELIA

Oh! Remorse is in my heart!
Tearing all my life apart,
here I see a brutal murderer,
there his victim, soon to die.

O rimorsi dell'amor
Che divorano il mio cor,
Fra un colpevole che sanguina
E la vittima che muor!

OSCAR

Aching grief beyond all bearing,
all around I see despairing!
See the pallor on his forehead there,
now his time has come to die!

O dolor senza misura!
O terribile sventura!
La sua fronte è tutta rorida
Già dell'ultimo sudor!

ANCKARSTROEM

Heaven! What madness! See, all
  around me
looks of hatred and of loathing!
Curse the fatal oath that bound me,
my suspicion was a lie!

Ciel! che feci! e che m'aspetta

Esecrato sulla terra! ...
Di qual sangue e qual vendetta
M'assetò l'infausto error!

GUSTAVUS

Hear me now: your King commands you:
I absolve and grant you pardon ...

Grazia a ognun: signor qui sono:
Tutti assolve il mio perdono ...

Ribbing and Horn are still at the back of the stage.

CHORUS

Hear his words of noble kindness,
save him, Lord, grant your forgiveness:
in Your mercy, Lord, look down on us,
Your great love do not deny.

[39] Cor sì grande e generoso
Tu ci serba, o Dio pietoso:
Raggio in terra a noi miserrimi
È del tuo celeste amor!

RIBBING AND HORN

Hear his words of noble kindness!

Core grande e generoso!

GUSTAVUS*

Farewell forever my children ...
farewell forever my land so dear
to me ... God bless you ...
God bless you! ...

Addio per sempre, miei figli ...
Addio, diletta America ... per
sempre ... Io moro! ... Ohimè!
Addio!

ALL

God help him,

Ei muore!

He makes one last effort and cries out. His voice fails him.
Lord God, forgive us all!   Notte d'

The curtain falls.

---

* Lit. 'Riccardo' bids farewell to America, his beloved.

Discography *by David Nice*

Conductor	T. Serafin	A. Votto	E. Leinsdorf	R. Muti
Orchestra/ Opera House	**Rome Opera**	**La Scala**	**RCA Italiana**	**New Philharmonia Orch. Royal Opera Chorus**
Date	*1943*	*1956*	*1967*	*1975*
Amelia	M. Caniglia	M. Callas	L. Price	M. Arroyo
Riccardo	B. Gigli	G. di Stefano	C. Bergonzi	P. Domingo
Renato	G. Bechi	T. Gobbi	R. Merrill	P. Cappuccilli
Ulrica	F. Barbieri	F. Barbieri	S. Verrett	F. Cossotto
Oscar	E. Ribetti	E. Ratti	R. Grist	R. Grist
Sam	T. Pasero	S. Maionica	E. Flagello	G. Howell
Tom	U. Novelli	N. Zaccaria	F. Mazzoli	R. Van Allan
UK LP Number	(EMI Italiana) 118392-3 (2)	(EMI) EX290925-3 (2)	—	(EMI) EX290710-3 (2)
UK Tape Number	(EMI Italiana) 118392-5 (2)	(EMI) EX290925-5 (2)	—	(EMI) EX290710-5 (2)
UK CD Number	—	(EMI) CDS7 47498-8 (2)	(RCA) GD86645 (2)	(EMI) CMS7 69576-2 (2)
US LP Number	(EMI Italiana) 118392-3 (3)	(EMI) EX290925-3 (2)	—	(EMI) EX290710-3 (2)
US Tape Number	(EMI Italiana) 118392-5 (2)	(EMI) EX290925-5 (2)	—	(EMI) EX290710-5 (2)
US CD Number	—	(EMI) CDS7 47498-8 (2)	(RCA) 6645-2 RG (2)	(EMI) CMS7 69576-2 (2)

Conductor	*C. Abbado*	*G. Solti*
Orchestra/Opera House	**La Scala**	**National PO** **London Opera Chorus**
Date	*1981*	*1985*
Amelia	K. Ricciarelli	M. Price
Riccardo	P. Domingo	L. Pavarotti
Renato	R. Bruson	R. Bruson
Ulrica	E. Obraztsova	C. Ludwig
Oscar	E. Gruberova	K. Battle
Sam	R. Raimondi	R. Lloyd
Tom	G. Foiani	M. King
UK LP Number	–	–
UK Tape Number	–	–
UK CD Number	(DG) 415 685-2GH2 (2)	(Decca) 410 210-2DH2 (2)
US LP Number	–	–
US Tape Number	–	–
US CD Number	(DG) 415 685-2GH2 (2)	(London) 410 210-2LH2 (2)

Selective Excerpts Number	Artists	LP Number	Tape Number	CD Number
Prelude	Sinopoli/VPO	–	–	(Philips) 411 469-2PH
Alla vita / Eri tu	B. Weikl	–	–	(Acanta) 43327
Alla vita / Eri tu	D. Fischer-Dieskau	(EMI) EX290432-3 (3)	(EMI) EX 290432-8 (3)	(EMI) CDH7 6 1053-2
Di' tu se fedele	J. Björling (r. 1944)	–	–	–
Di' tu se fedele / Ma se m'è forza perderti	P. Domingo	(DG) 2531 386	(DG) 3301 386	(DG) 415 366-2GH2
Ecco l'orrido campo	S. Dunn	–	(Decca) 421 420-4DH	(Decca) 421 420-2DH
Ecco l'orrido campo/ Morrò, ma prima in grazia	C. Vaness	(Nixa) NIX 1	(Nixa) NIXM 1	(Nixa) NIXC 1
Teco io sto (duet)	K. Ricciarelli/ P. Domingo (c. Gavazzeni)			
Eri tu	P. Amato (r. 1914)	(Preiser) CO430	–	(RCA) GD86534

There is a fascinating and discursive account of all the recordings issued before 1979 by Lord Harewood in *Opera on Record* (ed. Alan Blyth, Hutchinson, 1979). Although many are not currently available, this is an invaluable introduction to the wide variety of different interpretations of the opera.

Bibliography

An introduction to all Verdi's operas is admirably given in Julian Budden's *Verdi* in the Master Musicians series (Dent, 1985) and the longer analysis in volume two of his three-volume *The Operas of Verdi* (Cassell, 1984), is the best general survey of the opera in English. The enthusiastic perception of Gabriele Baldini's *The Story of Giuseppe Verdi*, trans. R. Parker, (Cambridge, 1980) is a splendid antidote to complacent assessment of the relative values of Verdi's works: he esteems *Un ballo in maschera* above all.

William Weaver's generously illustrated documentary study *Verdi* (London, 1977) contains much of the related correspondence, and more. Original chapters by F. Abbiati, F. Walker, F. Flora, G. Pannain, A. and N. Benois and M. Mila, among others, on performance history, the libretto, the staging, and the background to the composition of *Ballo*, make up the first three volumes of the Bolletino of the Istituto di Studi Verdiani, 1960, in English translation as well as Italian and German.

Elizabeth Forbes has written a vivid account of operatic life in Paris and London between 1830 and 1870 in *Mario and Grisi: a biography* (Gollancz, 1985) and 'The Age of Scribe at the Paris Opéra' in *Opera* (1968). There is no general survey of Somma's poetry or the art of the libretto in 19th-century Italy — apart from Patrick J. Smith's classic study, *The Tenth Muse: A Historical Study of the Opera Libretto* (London, 1971). John Rosselli's study of *The Opera Industry in Italy from Cimarosa to Verdi: The Role of the Impresario* (Cambridge, 1984) is a unique account of the practical difficulties of dealing with the censorship and managements.

Contributors

Pierluigi Petrobelli is Professor of Music in the University of Rome, and Director of the Istituto di Studi Verdiani, Parma.

Benedict Sarnaker is a lecturer in music at Goldsmiths' College, London.

Harold Powers is Professor of Music at Princeton University, New Jersey, and works on Italian opera, the music of India and the history of Western music theory.

David Nice, freelance writer and broadcaster, is the author of a forthcoming study of Richard Strauss (Omnibus, London).